GAME WON

HOW THE GREATEST HOME RUN EVER HIT SPARKED
THE 1988 DODGERS TO GAME ONE VICTORY
AND AN IMPROBABLE WORLD SERIES TITLE

STEVEN K. WAGNER

Mechanicsburg, PA USA

Published by Sunbury Press, Inc.
Mechanicsburg, PA USA

www.sunburypress.com

Copyright © 2021 by Steven K. Wagner.
Cover Copyright © 2021 by Sunbury Press, Inc.

Sunbury Press supports copyright. Copyright fuels creativity, encourages diverse voices, promotes free speech, and creates a vibrant culture. Thank you for buying an authorized edition of this book and for complying with copyright laws. Except for the quotation of short passages for the purpose of criticism and review, no part of this publication may be reproduced, scanned, or distributed in any form without permission. You are supporting writers and allowing Sunbury Press to continue to publish books for every reader. For information contact Sunbury Press, Inc., Subsidiary Rights Dept., PO Box 548, Boiling Springs, PA 17007 USA or legal@sunburypress.com.

For information about special discounts for bulk purchases, please contact Sunbury Press Orders Dept. at (855) 338-8359 or orders@sunburypress.com.

To request one of our authors for speaking engagements or book signings, please contact Sunbury Press Publicity Dept. at publicity@sunburypress.com.

FIRST SUNBURY PRESS EDITION: July 2021

Set in Adobe Garamond | Interior design by Crystal Devine | Cover by Lawrence Knorr | Edited by Lawrence Knorr.

Publisher's Cataloging-in-Publication Data
Names: Wagner, Steven K, author.
Title: Game won : how the greatest homerun ever hit sparked the 1988 Dodgers to a game one victory and an improbable world series title.
Description: In one swing of the bat, Game One—and, some say, the 1988 World Series itself—was over. *Game Won* relives the greatest home run ever hit, a blast by badly injured pinch hitter Kirk Gibson in the ninth-inning that propelled his weak-hitting Los Angeles Dodgers to a come-from-behind Game One miracle victory and an unlikely 1988 World Series title over the powerful Oakland A's.
Identifiers: ISBN : 978-1-62006-667-6 (softcover).
Subjects: SPORTS & RECREATION / Baseball / General | SPORTS & RECREATION / Baseball / History | SPORTS & RECREATION / Essays & Writings.

Product of the United States of America
0 1 1 2 3 5 8 13 21 34 55

Continue the Enlightenment!

Cover Photo: Kirk Gibson limps around the bases after hitting his historic home run. Photo by Joe Kennedy, (c) *Los Angeles Times*/TNS.

For Michelle and Hannah

CONTENTS

Foreword		vii
Acknowledgments		xiii
Prologue		xvii

CHAPTERS

1.	Game One	1
2.	The Rookie	17
3.	The Veteran	29
4.	First Blood – 2-0	34
5.	Slam – 4-2	45
6.	The Prelude	62
7.	The Calm	70
8.	Before the Storm	77
9.	Closing In – 4-3	82
10.	The Batboy	87
11.	Duel	98
12.	The Shot – 5-4	112

Afterword	124
Appendix	135
Notes	149
Index	152
About the Author	156

"NOT ONLY DID IT WIN THE GAME, [BUT KIRK GIBSON'S HOME RUN] PARALYZED THE A's AND WE WENT ON TO BEAT THEM IN FIVE GAMES AND WIN THE WORLD SERIES."

—Former Los Angeles Dodgers manager Tom Lasorda, recalling Gibson's ninth-inning home run against the Oakland A's in Game One of the 1988 World Series

FOREWORD

On June 15, 1968, senior Pat Kuehner, playing in his final college game, hit a two-strike, two-out, pinch-hit triple off the top of the wall, driving in two runners to overcome a 3-2 deficit and lead the University of Southern California Trojans to only the second walk-off victory in College World Series history and their fifth National Collegiate Athletic Association baseball championship. The hit represented the final college at-bat for Kuehner, who later served as an assistant coach on USC's 1971 and 1972 national championship teams and Arizona State University's 1977 NCAA championship squad.

There's nothing like Dodger Stadium in the fall. On most evenings, temperatures have cooled from the stifling late summer highs that typically buffet Los Angeles, and the hills surrounding the stadium stand like cathedrals. For fans, there's nothing finer than sitting in the bleachers, close to the fence and just beyond the outfield turf. A couple of feet closer and you might as well bring your spikes. So it was on October 15, 1988, during the World Series.

If we're given enough years on this earth, certain events that we either experience or that impact us become etched in our memories. Some are more localized in nature, while others are far-reaching, having broad implications to an entire community, country, or even the world. In some instances, we remember just where we were and what we were doing when significant events occurred.

Pat Kuehner

For me, the assassination of President Kennedy on November 22, 1963, is high on my list of life-impacting events, mainly due to the impact it had on our country and world. The president's death was followed five years later by the tragic death of his brother, Robert F. Kennedy, a candidate for president at the time he was killed. Both events affected me deeply and continue to impact our world more than half a century later.

On the sports side, the passing of a beloved man, USC baseball coach Rod Dedeaux, continues to resonate with me nearly 15 years later. Coach

Dedeaux, believed by many to have been the greatest college baseball coach ever, was a patient teacher and profound motivator during an impressionable period in my life, and his death in 2006 closed an era that was very dear to me.

Also significant from a sports standpoint is a baseball event so magnificent that it's difficult to fathom it three decades later: Kirk Gibson's miraculous home run that occurred late in the first game of the 1988 World Series, a game that spurred the Dodgers to a world championship. Like many others who were reared in Southern California, I recall it with great clarity.

Why do I remember that particular home run? Perhaps it's because I spent my formative years in Southern California and that during my college years I even played a time or two at Dodger Stadium, where Gibson's high-profile home run occurred on a warm Saturday evening to the delight of restless Dodger fans. Or, perhaps it's because I faced a similar situation in a high-profile baseball game exactly 20 years before Gibson did. The comparisons between Gibson's at-bat and one I had as a pinch-hitter for USC during the 1968 College World Series are eerily similar, giving me a unique perspective on batting in high-pressure situations. After Gibson hit his shot over the right-field wall my respect for him as a clutch hitter increased considerably.

First off, both of us were regular position players for our teams but neither started in either of those important games, Gibson due to a series of physical injuries and I to a different kind of "injury"—I had lost my brother just days before the College World Series began and was hitless in 14 at-bats over the four games we had played, probably due in part to a lack of concentration resulting from that tragedy. It was my last college game and the disappointment was palpable.

Both of us faced pitchers who used odd deliveries, with Gibson hitting against the Oakland Athletics' side-arm closer Dennis Eckersley and I challenging Southern Illinois University [SIU] left-hander Skip Pitlock, whose herky-jerky motion was difficult for hitters to follow and was a ticket to a short career in the minor leagues. Both of us were summoned off the bench with friendly encouragement from our field managers that went something like this: "Grab your gun, Tiger, and go hit one for us." That unique encouragement came from managers who were best of friends off the field: the legendary Tommy Lasorda and Rod Dedeaux, both of whom had played briefly for the Dodgers early on in their careers—Dedeaux in 1935 and Lasorda during the middle 1950s. Both of us had received scouting reports that told us exactly what pitch to expect when the going got the toughest and the game was on the line. When my moment of reckoning against SIU arrived, there were two strikes on me with two out in the bottom of the ninth inning; there were two men on base and our team was down by a run. Same scenario for Gibson.

Both Gibson and I collected only one hit during our respective series: I was 1 for 15, Gibson was 1 for 1. In his only at-bat Gibson hit a ball over the right-field fence to win the game, while I fell a foot short of clearing the right-field fence—that's where the comparison between the two of us ends.

There have been many landmark home runs in the history of major-league baseball. New York Giant Bobby Thomson's, which won a playoff series and sent his team to the 1951 World Series against the Yankees, which they lost, has long been considered by many the best ever. However, some consider veteran Bill Mazeroski's home run that won the seventh game of the 1960 World Series for the Pittsburgh Pirates the most important one ever hit. Carlton Fisk of the Boston Red Sox also hit a memorable smash to win Game Six of the 1975 World Series, a series they also lost. Of the four home runs—Thomson's, Mazeroski's, Fisk's, and Gibson's—only Mazeroski's and Gibson's helped their teams to world championships.

It is difficult to argue that Gibson's home run was not in the same elite category as Thomson's and Mazeroski's famous blasts, considering that Gibson had two badly injured legs, his drive was hit off a future MVP and Hall of Fame pitcher, and the at-bat was his only one of the World Series. Gibson's blast was indeed one of the very best—if not *the* very best—home runs ever hit.

Game Won explores that all-important first game of the 1988 World Series, held at a ballpark I once considered my own backyard. From aging veteran Mickey Hatcher's first-inning round-tripper that buoyed the Dodgers to an early 2-0 lead, to Jose Canseco's grand slam off the center-field camera that put Oakland ahead 4-2, to Gibson's dinger that won the game and sent Dodger fans into a delirium that still hasn't completely died down, *Game Won* is notable for one important reason. For the first time, Game One and the glory of Kirk Gibson's historic blast are explored in-depth, in book form. *Game Won* is an entire book about one ballgame, one very special ballgame.

The game *should* be explored in detail. Recent polls have shown Gibson's home run to be the most significant sports achievement in Los Angeles history and certainly in Dodger Stadium history. That it happened in one of the most significant sports cities anywhere in the entire world and during one of the most high-profile [and high-pressure!] of all sporting events speaks volumes about Gibson's place in Southern California history and the legacy he left when his baseball career ended.

Was it the greatest home run ever hit? It certainly could have been. Was Thomson's the greatest home run ever hit? It may have been. How about Mazeroski's? Perhaps it was. The beauty of sports and especially of individual sporting achievements is that greatness is often a subjective measurement. What one person believes to be the greatest home run, field goal, or golf shot ever achieved might only be considered second-best by another observer. Or perhaps third best.

Looking back through the retrospective of 33 years, there is little doubt about one thing: Game One of the 1988 World Series was a classic contest between two unique ball clubs, with the Oakland A's focusing on power and pitching and the Dodgers on smarts, stamina, and a vast armament of intangibles. It featured a player, Gibson, who had fire in his belly and was all business on the baseball diamond. It showed. In the end, the hare outran the tortoise. Little overpowered big. Good outlasted great. David bested Goliath. For the Los Angeles Dodgers on October 15, 1988, Game One truly was, as the title of this book suggests . . . *Game Won*.

—Pat Kuehner

ACKNOWLEDGMENTS

Words and photographs are the guts of any book, and my deep gratitude is due for the many hands that made my work as an author lighter, more concise, and more productive than it otherwise might have been. I am thankful to the following for their contributions to the preparation of this book. Without their assistance it would have been infinitely more challenging to complete this project and do justice to the players, managers, coaches, broadcasters, and others who made Game One among the most thrilling in World Series history:

- The *Los Angeles Times*, which provided the cover photograph that staff photographer Joe Kennedy shot as Kirk Gibson rounded the bases.
- Avis Mandel for granting permission to use his photograph of Vin Scully.
- Everett Raymond Kinstler, the National Portrait Gallery, and the Smithsonian Institution for allowing me to use Mr. Kinstler's portrait of Tommy Lasorda.
- The Carol M. Highsmith Archive, Library of Congress, for its aerial photograph of Dodger Stadium.
- The National Baseball Hall of Fame and Museum in Cooperstown, N.Y., for several of the photographs contained on these pages.

- The Athletic Communications office at Michigan State University for its photographs of Kirk Gibson.
- The University of Southern California for providing photographs of Mark McGwire and Vin Scully.
- Mount Vernon Nazarene University for its photographs of Tim Belcher.
- Bowling Green University for providing a photograph of Orel Hershiser.
- Oklahoma University for making available a photograph of Mickey Hatcher.
- Brad Kuehfuss for photographing his Game One ticket stub.
- The Baseball Almanac and Baseball-Reference.com, whose statistical data was instrumental in defining many of the players described herein.

A special thanks goes to the dozens of managers, coaches, ballplayers, executives, broadcasters, and fans who were willing to share with me their thoughts on Game One and the home run that abruptly ended it—the greatest home run ever hit. The recollections of each were essential in helping me paint a picture of a baseball game that occurred more than 30 years ago but is etched in the collective memories of each contributor:

Tom Lasorda, manager of the 1988 world championship Los Angeles Dodgers and winner of two World Series

Rick Honeycutt, the former Dodger pitching coach, a former American League all-star, and a member of the Dodger pitching staff in 1987 and the A's pitching staff in 1988

Fred Claire, former Dodgers general manager and architect of the 1988 championship squad

Mike Davis, hero number two of Game One

Batting coach Ben Hines, who helped orchestrate the Dodgers' hitting success in 1988

Third base coach Joe Amalfitano, who was a fixture with the Dodgers for 16 years and the first person to excitedly smack Gibson's hand as he rounded the bases

A's first base coach Rene Lachemann, who formerly managed the Seattle Mariners, Milwaukee Brewers, Florida Marlins, and Chicago Cubs.

Former American League batting champion Carney Lansford, an all-star for the Oakland A's in 1988

Rick Dempsey, World Series MVP in 1983 and the Dodgers' backup catcher in 1988

Oakland relief pitcher Greg Cadaret, who warmed up prior to Dennis Eckersley's fateful appearance in Game One

Ricky Horton, a member of the Dodgers' coveted 1988 relief staff and a longtime St. Louis Cardinals broadcaster

Dodgers' utility player Tracy Woodson, now the head baseball coach at his hometown University of Richmond in Virginia

Bill Virdon, National League Rookie of the Year in 1955, former manager of the Pittsburgh Pirates, New York Yankees, Houston Astros, and Montreal Expos, and an eyewitness to Bill Mazeroski's famous 1960 World Series home run

Carl Erskine, author of two no-hitters, a member of the Brooklyn Dodgers' 1955 world championship team, an all-star with the Dodgers in 1954, and an eyewitness to Bobby Thomson's 1951 "shot heard 'round the world."

Former Dodger Irv Noren, a member of the 1954 American League all-star team that competed against Erskine and his National League all-star teammates.

Mike Cameron, an all-star with the Seattle Mariners and one of only 18 men to hit four home runs in a single game

Pat Kuehner, hero of the 1968 College World Series for NCAA champion University of Southern California and assistant coach for Arizona State's 1977 NCAA championship baseball team

Laurie Lachemann, wife of then-A's first-base coach Rene Lachemann.

Jason Arellano, Susan Colias, Craig and Scott Dondanville, Careen Jones, Brad Kuehfuss, the late Glade Merkley, Keith Merkley, Ross Peabody, Rob and Evan Wagner, and Kathy Willett, all of whom attended Game One of the 1988 World Series and provided eyewitness accounts.

None left the game early.

PROLOGUE

[Kirk Gibson] . . . will not see any action tonight, for sure. —Los Angeles Dodgers announcer Vin Scully's declaration during the eighth inning of Game One[1]

On a summer day in 1960, my father piled his sons into our family car and motored 20 miles to a ballpark that was then under construction at a place we'd never heard of called Chavez Ravine, which was situated in a humble barrio just off the Pasadena Freeway and west of downtown Los Angeles. A year earlier, on September 17, 1959, my parents had piloted us to the same locale, the future site of Dodger Stadium. Later that day, in that barren landscape, a groundbreaking celebration would be hosted by the Los Angeles Dodgers. Some 3,000 people were on hand that day, parking in and around the prospective infield, and my family was among the first to arrive. In some respects, we never left.

Dodger Stadium, which would loosely replicate Holman Stadium, the Dodgers' spring training ballpark in Vero Beach, Florida, was a dirt pit on the day of our 1960 foray into history, a mass of concrete, steel, cast iron, lumber, and hardware so chaotic and incomplete that it hardly resembled a sports theater at all, let alone the future home to one of baseball's greatest franchises.

Decked in Keds and cuffed jeans, my brother and I trod the sprawling grounds with lively exuberance, gazing wide-eyed upon the great dusty expanse and envisioning a playground where lush turf, pallid bases, cluttered dugouts, endless grandstands, and strident cheers for the home team would one day collide in perfect harmony. On that warm Southern California afternoon we could almost see Gil Hodges stretch at first base for a hurried throw from third baseman and Brooklyn holdover Jim "Junior" Gilliam, who would die young. Or the "Duke of [formerly] Flatbush" Snider, who would die old, race in to snag a low line drive off the bat of some unknown Milwaukee Brave, perhaps the great Hank Aaron or Eddie Matthews. And righty Clem Labine, a two-time all-star who led the National League in saves in 1956 and 1957? In my mind's eye he resembled a thoroughbred, reaching from the mound toward home plate like Man of War at the finish line and snapping his sturdy wrist to spin a hanging curveball 60 feet, six inches toward catcher John Roseboro, who by then was a mainstay crouched inside a chalk-lined box behind home plate, similar to one that Roy Campanella occupied in Brooklyn for a decade of years. That is, until a tragic car accident left him permanently paralyzed and ended his dazzling career.

No one was certain where the other players would fit on this imagined team and presumed ballfield, because in 1960 the new—names like Wills and Fairly and Davis and Howard—were beginning to encroach upon the old, folks like Erskine and Furillo and Amoros and even former Yankee Irv Noren, whose 1960 season would be his first in Dodger flannels but his last as a player.

"It's the most gorgeous thing I've seen in my life," said shortstop and soon-to-be Most Valuable Player Maury Wills, describing Dodger Stadium shortly before it opened. "The infield is perfect. It's nice and firm and true. It's bound to get better, too. They've done a wonderful job on it."[2]

With a certain finality, we meandered over to the hulking concrete frame of what eventually would become the Dodger Stadium broadcast booth, a prime vantage point where *he* would eventually sit game after glorious game, season after endless season, decade after long decade with his trusted colleague, Jerry Doggett, the duo then calling games for radio station KFI, which proudly boasted to its faithful listeners across the expansive Southland and beyond: "50,000 watts, day or night." The booth would be Vin Scully's to occupy from 1962, the team's first season at Dodger Stadium, through 2016, Scully's last, just as a booth 3,000 miles away in a place called Brooklyn was his to inhabit from 1950 through 1957 at Ebbets Field and from 1958 through 1961 at the Los Angeles Memorial Coliseum, which the Dodgers called home while Dodger Stadium was under construction.

In 1960, the 33-year-old Scully was already a broadcast legend, a microphonic fixture so complete and beloved that he would inhabit a broadcast booth, for CBS Radio but mostly for the Brooklyn and Los Angeles Dodgers, for the better part of a century—67 years in all, longer than any other big-time sports announcer. And when the sand trickling through his hour glass would begin to ebb with a long-dreaded-but-inevitable retirement announcement before the 2016 season began, the team would fondly reconfigure its home address in his honor: 1000 Elysian Park Avenue fittingly became 1000 Vin Scully Avenue, Los Angeles, California, 90090. Then, the legend behind the golden mic, the man with the elysian voice, quietly disappeared into a pink California sunset, confining himself to rare special appearances. Gone from the airwaves was his famous signature greeting, inviting listeners, at least for that evening, into the world of Dodger baseball: *Hi, everybody, and a very pleasant good evening to you, wherever you may be . . .*

Not before leaving a historical legacy.

That legacy included several landmark calls from the bunker-like future broadcast booth that my brother and I so eagerly traversed that afternoon in 1960. First, there was Dodger Stadium's opening game, on April 10, 1962, with pitcher Johnny Podres, hero of the team's only Brooklyn world championship in 1955, on the mound. The Dodgers would lose that first game at Dodger Stadium, but they'd find their winning ways the very next day against Cincinnati and end up in the World Series the following season. Later, on September 9, 1965, Scully would broadcast Sandy Koufax's perfect game, also at Dodger Stadium. "Swung on and missed, a perfect game!" Scully breathlessly declared as San Francisco's Harvey Kuehn struck out swinging to end the one-sided contest with a Giant whimper. It was

Aerial view of Dodger Stadium (Carol M. Highsmith Archive, Library of Congress).

also Koufax who had won the fourth and final game of the 1963 World Series, a game called by—who else?—Scully. With the win, the Dodgers had swept—indeed, humiliated—a Yankee baseball machine that boasted such luminaries as three-time MVP Mickey Mantle, three-time MVP Yogi Berra, MVP and then-single-season home run king Roger Maris, that season's MVP Elston Howard, and former Cy Young Award winner Whitey Ford. To their credit, the Dodgers fielded a team that included former MVP Wills, MVP and eventual three-time Cy Young Award winner Sandy Koufax, former Cy Young Award winner Don Drysdale, and consecutive years—1962 and 1963—batting champ Tommy Davis. Not to mention the greatest announcer in sports history, the timeless and venerable Scully, who already was one of the all-time greats.

As the belletristic Scully might put it, the piece de resistance came on October 15, 1988, when, during the first game of the World Series against the powerful Oakland Athletics, he had the good fortune to call what some believe is the greatest moment in Dodger Stadium history. On that day, with his team trailing 4-3 in the bottom of the ninth inning, the injured Kirk Gibson strode confidently to home plate with two out and a runner on first base. With the Dodgers gasping for breath and the right-field fence appearing to stretch across the Chavez Ravine landscape miles from where he stood next to home plate, Gibson promptly muscled a historic home run to win the game, sending shock waves from Los Angeles to Oakland and across the country. "High fly ball into right field, she is . . . GONE!" Scully affirmed after Gibson sent a Dennis Eckersley back-door slider sailing just beyond the reach of right fielder Jose Canseco, over the sky-blue corrugated metal fence and several rows into the cheap seats, known to Dodger fans as "The Pavilion." Moments later, after the thunderous cheers of 55,983 fans had finally subsided in a decrescendo, Scully offered his listening audience a long-remembered epilogue, one that echoes today: "In a year that has been so improbable, the impossible has happened." The home run marked Gibson's only appearance in the 1988 World Series, and he would never again play in a Fall Classic.

Gibson's blast certainly wasn't the first landmark home run that Scully had announced in his long and eventful career, not even at Dodger Stadium. On April 8, 1974, he broadcast Hank Aaron's 715th career home run in Los Angeles. That shot broke Babe Ruth's longstanding mark of 714 and elevated Aaron, who was followed from short to third on his home run trot by gleeful fans patting him on the back, to the top spot as the all-time greatest home run hitter ever. He was also on hand when Hodges, who would be deprived of Hall of Fame status, hit four home runs against the Boston Braves on August 31, 1950; more than half a century later, on May 21, 2002, he would watch from his perch high above the playing field as Dodger Shawn Green, a sinewy slugger with the power of Zeus, hit four balls out of the park against the Milwaukee Brewers in a six-hit game that set a new major-league record for total bases.

The granddaddy of them all, dubbed the "shot heard 'round the world," occurred on October 3, 1951, in New York's Polo Grounds. Scully was working alongside iconoclastic Brooklyn announcer Red Barber as part of a broadcast team that included Connie Desmond. However, the youthful Scully wasn't the lead play-by-play man when Bobby Thomson of the New York Giants, in the first nationally televised baseball game, came to bat against the Dodgers in the final game of a playoff series

Vin Scully (© Avis Mandel).

with the pennant on the line. With his team trailing 3-1, Thomson hit a dramatic ninth-inning three-run home run off Ralph Branca to win the game and series and send the Giants dancing into the World Series, with echoes of Giants announcer Russ Hodges declaring, "The Giants win the pennant, the Giants win the pennant, the Giants win the pennant, the Giants win the pennant" ringing in their ears. The home run was widely considered the greatest in baseball history, although all that would change on October 15, 1988.

"It was the best thing that ever happened to me," Thomson once told an inquiring reporter many years after his historic blast. "It may have been the best thing that ever happened to anybody."[3]

Thomson's thrilling homer aside, there have been other memorable blasts in the entirety of baseball history, such Bill Mazeroski's walk-off home run that won the 1960 World Series for the Pittsburgh Pirates. Some believe Mazeroski, who nearly flew around the bases at Forbes Field in Pittsburgh, one-upped the three-time all-star Thomson by hitting *his* home run to win the Series; Thomson "merely" won a pennant.

"When I hit second [base], I don't think I touched the ground all the way to home plate," Mazeroski said, something film of the blast almost confirms. He added, "I never dreamed that something like this would happen."[4]

And who could forget Carlton Fisk of the Boston Red Sox who, with his team facing elimination in Game Six of the 1975 World Series, willed and waved and danced into fair territory a blast hit down the left-field line in the bottom of the 12th inning to break a 6-6 tie and give his team the victory. Boston would lose Game Seven the following day despite the blast and with that the World Series itself to the Cincinnati Reds, then known as the Big Red Machine.

Thirty-three years later, Gibson's home run continues to resonate with fans everywhere, especially in Los Angeles, where Gibson truly left his mark. It was, I believe, the greatest in baseball history. Here's why.

For starters, Gibson was injured that day, and his movement and ability to practice before Game One were limited. Second, *both* of his legs were hurting, his right one due to a swollen knee and his left one due to a hamstring injury—he was unable to push off his left foot or land on his right when striding toward a pitched ball. Third, because Gibson was injured, he had spent most of the ballgame either in the dugout or in the clubhouse being attended to by trainers, rendering him unable to loosen up. Fourth, when it came time to bat he was literally as cold as the ice that had cooled his legs up to and including the dramatic ninth inning. Fifth, Gibson was forced to bat against Oakland A's closer Dennis Eckersley, one of the best pitchers in the American League and perhaps one of the greatest pitchers in baseball history. Eckersley, a former 20-game winner, would lead the league in saves that year with 45 and win both an MVP Award and a Cy Young Award four years later. Sixth, early in his six-minute at-bat Gibson dribbled a squibber down the first base line, forcing a labored dash toward first base before the ball was declared foul—a sprint that exacerbated the pain. Seventh, Gibson's home run set the tone for the rest of the Series. The result was that the powerful A's folded their tents early and essentially closed shop—rather than take a 1-0 World Series lead, Oakland would also lose Game Two against the Dodgers, head home trailing two games to none, and lose two of the next three games and the Series despite having a 21-game winner, Dave Stewart, and two of the league's top four home run hitters: Jose Canseco, at number one with 42, and Mark McGwire, at number four with 32. In contrast, the Dodgers had nobody hitting .300 or higher on the season, no player with more than 25 home runs [Gibson], and no one with more than 82 runs batted in [first baseman Mike Marshall]. Finally, magnifying the seriousness of his lower extremity condition, the home run at-bat was Gibson's only appearance in the World Series. After hitting the game-winner, on top of two home runs in the National League Championship Series, the badly hobbled Gibson appeared nearly unable to complete the requisite trot around the bases.

In contrast, Thomson's blast came against Ralph Branca, a lifetime .564 pitcher who lost 12 games in 1951 and who would win just 88 games in a career that would see him earn no appreciable awards. Mazeroski's home run would come off another Ralph, Ralph Terry, a career .519 pitcher who was 10-8 in 1960 and whose lifetime 3.62 earned run average was decent at best but well short of spectacular. While Mazeroski's home run won a World Series for the Pirates, there was nothing else unusual about it other than the fact that it won a World Series. Both Thomson and Mazeroski were healthy, well-warmed, and facing average pitchers at the moment they blasted their way into baseball immortality; Gibson faced a pitching demon. Although Gibson's home run won Game One, it effectively won the entire World Series.

Game Won is the story of "Game One" and the nine innings that set the tone for the 1988 World Series, a unique matchup that 33 years later still has baseball historians scratching their heads. It's the story of a player who shouldn't have played, a home run that shouldn't have soared, a World Series matchup that resoundingly favored Oakland, who on paper dominated the Dodgers offensively and whose 3.44 team earned run average was only slightly higher than the Dodgers' collective and league-leading ERA of 2.96, and a team that shouldn't have won. It's also a testament to how one well-hit bomb, propelled exclusively by one man's arms and described by one fan as having a "seven-game impact," could quickly tame a team that had entered Dodger Stadium with their heads held high but who exited after Game Two with their tails between their collective legs. Those tails would drag for three more games, with Oakland only winning Game Three, 2-1, on a ninth-inning home run by McGwire. After winning Games One and Two, the Dodgers would lose Game Three, narrowly win Game Four, and less narrowly win Game Five. *Finis.*

What about Gibson, who was just past the midpoint of his more-than-respectable career? After winning the National League's MVP Award in 1988 with just 25 home runs and 76 RBI, he would hit nine home runs the following season, eight in 1990, and his career as a Dodger would be over. Before Gibson would call it quits, four more lukewarm seasons would follow, with Kansas City, Pittsburgh, and Detroit. He hit 175 home runs before the famous dinger and just 80 afterward.

Still, Gibson's legacy is secure. His World Series home run is invariably acknowledged as a favorite of fans and an all-time great blast in media evaluations that every so often examine its historical significance in the context of other baseball achievements. Even the players respect it as one of the best home runs ever, rivaling those of Thomson, Mazeroski, Fisk, and others.

Perhaps ex-Dodger Noren, whose career began the year before Thomson's mighty blast and who himself clocked 65 round-trippers before retiring as a Dodger in 1960, put Gibson's home run in the best possible perspective, hinting it may have been the most spectacular one ever hit, all things considered. Said Noren, who was then 94: "It was great, it was unbelievable. It had to be one of the best [home runs ever] considering [everything]. It was certainly one of the best *I've* seen."

For my 1960 excursion to Chavez Ravine, aka Dodger Stadium, the prime mover was a neighbor who installed the turf there. I recall with amusement that the man once treated his own parched lawn with a green substance that lent it color and vibrancy—paint, the neighborhood kids laughingly called it. On opening day, the turf at Dodger Stadium displayed an unusually deep verdant hue. Scully later attributed that to a technique that the movie industry employed to color thirsty hills for movie shoots. The methodology involved adding vegetable dye to the grass, which enhanced it. The dye was used because owner Walter O'Malley feared recent torrential rains in the Los Angeles area would deplete the stadium of its lush turf. His fears were misguided, and the *bocage*—even the ballpark's darkened grass—was beautiful to observe from top to bottom.

"Even when I saw the plans and watched the park grow, I still can't believe it," the late Baseball Commissioner Ford Frick said at the time the stadium opened. "It's like a dream come true."[5]

I'm not certain there's a connection between my neighbor's effort to paint his lawn and Hollywood's vegetable dye ingenuity, but Dodger Stadium eventually got it right and the grass turned the fertile green that it is today—naturally. The legacy of Game One also matured, and today it's even stronger than it was back then. The players have all moved on, some to positions inside baseball but many to *real* jobs or even retirement. Unlike them, Game One has remained frozen in time, a testament to the gutsiness of the injured Gibson and the prowess of his scrappy, blue-collar teammates.

For this book I interviewed witnesses to what most believe are the three greatest home runs ever hit: former Brooklyn Dodger Carl Erskine, now 94, who was warming up in the bullpen when Thomson hit his "Shot Heard 'Round the World" to clinch the 1951 National League pennant; former Pittsburgh Pirate Bill Virdon, 90, who was awaiting his turn at bat when Bill Mazeroski homered to win the 1960 World Series; and, among others, former Los Angeles Dodger Mike Davis, who was standing on second base when Gibson homered and who scored the tying run as the slugger circled the bases to win the game. As expected, there was no consensus among the three about which was the greatest home run ever hit. My money is on Gibson.

While the glory of Game One continues to sparkle in the minds of baseball historians, the passage of time has been less sympathetic to subsequent Dodger teams, which have struggled in the post-season on more than one occasion under the critical eye of a news media that have little patience for failure. The organization, which averaged a World Series title every two and one-half years between its first one against the New York Yankees in 1955 and its fourth one against the Minnesota Twins in 1965 and every five years between 1955 and the stunner of 1988, finally won its first world championship since that 1988 knockout of Oakland in 2020, much to the delight of fans and the media. Many believe the 1988 title spurred the team on in 2020, that players and management were simply fed up with hearing about 1988 as "the last time." Now, for the Dodgers, the last time was 2020. Still, the 1988 World Series remains to many baseball fans a historical signpost toward a moment in time worth revisiting—and to the Los Angeles Dodgers a Game Won.

—SKW

CHAPTER I

GAME ONE

For the longest time, my parents had four season seats right behind home plate at Dodger Stadium. As a result, we were able to get playoff and World Series tickets, and that's how I was able to go [to Game One]. I went with my mom, my dad, and my younger brother

We were directly behind home plate, maybe 15 rows up. When Mickey Hatcher homered I was feeling pretty good, but it didn't last long. After Canseco hit the grand slam, things weren't looking that great. But I'm always hopeful, and when you listened to Vinnie [Scully], there was always hope in his voice. He was always optimistic. Back then, everyone brought radios to the games. They would play them loud and you could hear Vinnie throughout the stadium.

[In the ninth inning] I thought we were in trouble, especially when the first two guys got out. Luckily, Eckersley walked [Mike Davis]. People in the crowd were wondering, "What's next?" Then, the greatest thing happened.

I was always looking into the dugout because we sat close enough. I could see Lasorda and then a commotion of some kind, and all of a sudden Gibson walked out. The crowd went crazy. He walked out a few steps, his head was down, he took a couple of swings, and now here we go. I was thinking, "Wow—he can hardly walk." You never know what can happen.

I thought, "Hit the ball somewhere." I wasn't thinking home run because [with the injuries] he didn't have the power to hit a home run. Then it happened. It was a good home run, but it didn't go out by a lot.

Everyone stood up and there was a nonstop ovation. It was pretty amazing, pretty exciting. This was by far the number one sporting event I've ever been to. It was something I'll never forget. —Craig Dondanville, 63, Bullhead City, Arizona

---

A light breeze strafed the outfield pavilion as a woman named Gibson stepped slowly to a microphone, stood between dueling 395-foot markers painted symmetrically on a sky-blue corrugated metal outfield fence, and calmly vocalized a wholesome rendition of the National Anthem while players with the Los Angeles Dodgers and Oakland A's lined both base paths and 50,000 nervous fans looked on approvingly. The lost irony, rediscovered more than 30 years later, is that Debbie Gibson would be one of two Gibsons making a splash that day at Dodger Stadium, the other coming nine innings later as a red glare, not of rockets but of taillights guided by fans exiting the stadium in advance of what they expected would be a Game One World Series loss, glimmered in the distance.

"So the Dodgers brought in Debbie Gibson, if only they had *Kirk* Gibson," lamented CBS Radio announcer Bill White before Scully and Joe Garagiola assumed their television broadcast duties for Game One.[1] Little did White know that the aching outfielder would soon supplant the vibrant singer/songwriter as the most important Gibson to appear at Dodger Stadium on that memorable day.

It is well known, at least locally, that Dodger fans frequently leave the stadium early if a game is one-sided, hoping to dodge a vast crowd exiting the parking lot en masse and a mad vehicular dash for the nearby Pasadena, Golden State, and 101 freeways. Most simply hope to arrive home at a reasonable hour in anticipation of an early-morning wakeup and a challenging drive to work via the frenzied Los Angeles freeway system. Whatever their rationale, that evening was no exception, and those who departed prematurely missed a dramatic, if not franchise-changing, event.

Rob Wagner, a Los Angeles-based financial services recruiter, nearly left the ballpark before the game was over. According to Wagner, a lifelong Dodger fan who began following the team in the 1950s, he contemplated leaving before the ninth inning in hopes of avoiding the bottleneck of cars that would exit the stadium immediately after what appeared would be a 4-3 Dodger loss in Game One. However, his inclination was redirected by his six-year-old son Evan, who insisted they stay until the final out was recorded. It never was:

> "I got the tickets that morning from a guy in my office. He got them from a minority owner of the Dodgers. They were very good seats, ground level along the first-base line—maybe 15 rows back, real good tickets. I had very early hours at work the next morning, maybe 5:00 or 5:30. I wanted to leave the game in the eighth inning, and I told Evan that we had to get going to beat the traffic, but he just insisted we stay—which he has never ceased to remind me. I begrudgingly agreed to stay, and I'm glad I did. Finally, we walked out into the parking lot and people were still cheering 20 or 30 minutes later—they refused to leave the stadium. The ovation went on and on and on. It was cool."

As expected, tickets such as Wagner's—indeed, most tickets—went for premium prices as the morning of Game One approached, largely due to the huge demand created by the team's unexpected playoff victory over the Mets only days earlier. The price tag for the most expensive seats in the house eventually increased tenfold over the original sticker price to near extortionate levels.

The best seats, field boxes behind home plate and along the first- and third-base lines, sold for $750 compared with a listed price on tickets of $50. The worst seats, in the pavilions behind the right- and left-field fences and higher up toward the top of the stadium, sold for $100. The listed cost of bleacher, reserved, and general admission seats was less than half that—$40.

The first opportunity to buy World Series and playoff ducats went to fans who held season tickets. The Dodgers said at the time that an estimated 41,000 tickets were distributed to those faithful. Another 2,500 to 3,000 tickets for each game were awarded to fans through a lottery held in the summer.

The team also distributed more than 400 tickets for each World Series game through the sales and distribution companies Ticketron and Ticketmaster, with all tickets in the hands of fans within two hours. At that time, those two companies were virtually the only games in town for fans who wished to purchase tickets to high-profile sporting, musical, and other events.

The origin of Game One dates back three days before the opening pitch when, on October 12, 1988, the Dodgers beat the New York Mets 6-0, thanks to a gem thrown by pitcher Orel Hershiser. Buoyed by nine singles and a double, Hershiser threw a five-hit, complete-game shutout to win Game Seven and send his team careening into the World Series after closing the book on a National League Championship Series that many people figured they would handily lose, possibly in four games.

For good reason. The Mets had Darryl Strawberry at the peak of his career, and the Los Angeles native had posted a league-leading 39 home runs and 101 RBI, tops on his team in both categories that season—the former mark tying his career high; no Dodger came close to matching either offensive statistic. Scully would follow former first lady Nancy Reagan's toss of the first pitch by urging youngsters to heed the admonition of her anti-drug campaign, dubbed "Just Say No." By the end of Game One, most of those in attendance had a high no drug could inspire.

The Mets also had a dominant pitching rotation that consisted of David Cone, 20-3 with a 2.22 ERA; Dwight Gooden, 18-9 with a 3.19; and Ron Darling, 17-9 with a 3.25. Bob Ojeda, at 2.88, and Sid Fernandez, 3.03, rounded out the regular-season rotation, with all five starters winning in double figures. A team ERA of 2.91 and a team batting average of .256 with a collective 152 home runs compared favorably with the Dodgers' 2.96 ERA and .248 batting average with just 99 home runs, one-fourth of them powered by one player: the hurting-and-therefore-unavailable, it was presumed, Gibson.

Even Dodger first baseman Mike Marshall was a skeptic going into the series, conceding later that the Mets had more talent but the Dodgers were better during their seven-game series. Why? The team believed in itself.

Dodger reliever Jay Howell shared that sentiment, saying the team knew it was second-best and it would have to play its heart out to win the series. The key, Howell said, was to rally around two guys: Gibson and Hershiser, with the other players following their lead.

Second baseman Steve Sax made it unanimous, saying he enjoyed being the underdog. Sax said that puts the pressure to win on the other team, giving the Dodgers the feeling they had everything to win since the expectation was that they would lose.

For six games the series was see-saw, with the Mets winning Game One, the Dodgers Game Two, the Mets Game Three, the Dodgers Games Four and Five, and the Mets Game Six before Hershiser, perhaps the best pitcher in baseball at that time with a 23-8 mark and a record 59 consecutive scoreless innings at one juncture, put the skids on things with his masterful outing. The key to the team's success occurred late in Game Four. With the Mets ahead in the series, 2-1, and Gooden cruising along in the ninth inning, 4-2, Dodgers catcher Mike Scioscia blasted a two-run home run over the center-field fence to send the game into extra innings. Gibson put the Dodgers ahead for good with a solo shot in the top of the 12th inning that tied the series at 2-2 and virtually ended any hope the Mets had of taking a 3-1 series lead into Game Five at their home ballpark, Shea Stadium, and ultimately winning the series. Instead, the Dodgers also won Game Five, a victory that sent the series back to Los Angeles, where the team needed only a split of the remaining two

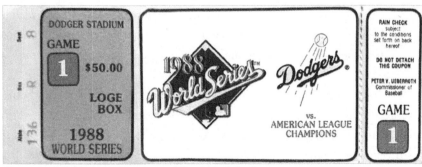

Game One ticket stub (courtesy of Brad Kuehfuss).

games to earn a spot in the World Series. Hershiser's victory in Game Seven assured his teammates of that prize.

"I had no idea I could shut them out on only two days rest," Hershiser said after Game Seven. "My mechanics were very bad for about the first two or three innings . . . Finally, I got into a groove and made some adjustments." Added manager Tom Lasorda: "Nobody thought we could win. When we went to spring training, they said, 'The Dodgers are through.' Restoring the tradition of this organization is a great thrill.

"We beat the best team in the National League, man for man. Everyone believed [we couldn't win] but the players."[2]

While Hershiser excelled, utility player Mickey Hatcher persisted, adding a personal dose of *élan vital*. He played superbly. The questions raised by his play would uplift eyebrows today—more than three decades after the fact.

> "Haven't they done enough?" asked *Los Angeles Times* columnist Scott Ostler. "Can they possibly get any higher, happier, or soggier? How can any two teams top the events of this series? Games played in the rain and mud . . . Inflammatory newspaper columns . . . Extra-inning thrills . . . Crimes committed before a national TV audience . . . Great pitching performances . . . The fielding collapse of the century . . . They can't play a World Series right now. This is too tough an act to follow. This was such a big game [Game Seven]. Kirk Gibson shaved before it started. You don't get any bigger than that. Besides, it's going to take us experts at least two weeks just to figure out how the Dodgers managed to beat the Mets. It's the mystery of the year, at least, and we have to unravel the clues, analyze the stats and examine the lab tests on the pine tar."[3]

As the Dodgers took the field for Game One of the World Series, Scully waxed coincidental: "It is ironic that the Dodgers, in waiting before the first ball to be thrown out, showed some highlights of both the season and the league championship series, and the bulk of the highlights [involved] the dramatic contributions of Kirk Gibson, who will not be in the starting lineup and was not introduced," Scully said. "He was back in the trainer's room getting some aid." He then asked rhetorically, "If you're the manager, Tommy Lasorda, how do you feel about losing your biggest gun?"

The consigliere Lasorda, speaking in a pre-recorded interview that was broadcast before Game One, responded in an almost conversational fashion to Scully's question, "In my opinion, I think Kirk Gibson should be the most valuable player in the National League."

Scully had said several hours earlier that Lasorda had commented on the Dodger trainers, who were working with Gibson to apparently get him ready for the game, if that were even possible, and they seemed "loose" and appeared to be kidding around when they indicated to him that the star would not play. When asked by Scully to elaborate, the manager responded that he believed his slugger *would* see action.[4] Indeed he would, action that would shake the ballpark to its foundation.

Constructed between 1959 and 1962 as a means of officially completing the recently transplanted Brooklyn Dodgers' transition out of the cavernous Los Angeles Memorial Coliseum and into their new headquarters several miles from downtown Los Angeles, Dodger Stadium is a baseball anomaly and one of the three oldest major-league baseball stadiums, its rivals for that honor being Fenway Park in Boston and Wrigley Field, home of the Chicago Cubs. Situated in the heart of Chavez Ravine and within eyeshot of the picturesque and occasionally snow-capped San Gabriel Mountains, dubbed the "good mountains" by writer John Steinbeck, the stadium affords fans a soothing view of dancing palms and the low hills that meander through one of many barrios that dot Los Angeles County. There are no downtown high rises to crowd the stadium, no effective public transportation system to reel in fans, and no nearby restaurants to accommodate spectators before a typical 7:10 P.M. weekday start time. There's only baseball, and since it opened during the Kennedy administration, Dodger Stadium and the team it so faithfully accommodates have entertained 150 million fans.

The team has called Dodger Stadium, considered by many the most beautiful ballpark in America, home for 59 years, a relationship that began in 1957 when Dodgers owner Walter O'Malley, an emphatic baseball visionary, failed to convince the powers that be in Brooklyn to build a replacement for legendary, but aging, Ebbets Field. As a result, O'Malley packed up his team of stars and moved out West, where major-league baseball had up until then been merely a pipe dream, fodder for conversation. Along with O'Malley and the players came timeless announcer Scully, a Bronx native, Fordham University graduate, and almost-favorite son due to the school's proximity between his hometown and Brooklyn. Once in Southern California, the club would eventually inhabit roughly 300 acres given to it by the city of Los Angeles in a swap for old Wrigley Field, once home to the minor-league Los Angeles Angels and a minor-league baseball venue for three decades.

Groundbreaking occurred on September 17, 1959, with large earthmovers sweeping down steep slopes where the stands would someday reside, shoving dirt and rocks ahead of them as 3,000 fans, who on that day parked in and around what eventually would become the playing field, looked on. The infield dirt was chalked to guide the imagination of spectators, and players were stationed at imaginary bases—quickly to be enveloped by autograph seekers. The ceremony, as always, was first class.

Opened on April 10, 1962, the ballpark, built for roughly $23 million, quickly developed—and has maintained—a reputation for cleanliness and beauty. Even so, the seating capacity hasn't changed much: roughly 56,000 fans may enjoy that beauty in any given game, the same approximate number that could experience a game—and it *is* an experience—on opening day in 1962. Memorable baseball moments in the stadium's history include the mob of players, led by a host of Steves—relief pitcher Howe, catcher Yeager, and first baseman Garvey—hugging and back-slapping each other on the pitcher's mound after winning the 1981 World Series.

"The mound is real good, I like it," Dodger pitcher Johnny Podres said before the opening. "This park knocks your eyes out."[5] Podres, hero of the 1955 World Series, the team's only championship in Brooklyn before heading west to California, was as representative an analyst as anyone.

Little has changed in that regard over half a century. The ballpark is still as beautiful and functional as it was back then. The field dimensions haven't changed much, either, measuring a cozy 330 feet down the lines and 400 feet to dead center field.

Through the years, Dodger Stadium has seen numerous baseball generations come and go, including Fernando-mania in the early 1980s, Nomo-mania in the 1990s, and the era of Kershaw, believed by many to be among the greatest pitchers who ever lived as evidenced by the three Cy Young awards he won, in 2011, 2013 and 2014, and 21-win seasons in 2011 and 2014. Between the three of them, Fernando Valenzuela, Hideo Nomo, and Clayton Kershaw threw three no-hitters during their careers, Valenzuela's coming in 1990, Nomo's in 1996, and Kershaw's in 2014—all of them called by Scully. Add to that four by Koufax, including his perfect game against the Cubs, and a smattering of others—Bill Singer, Jerry Reuss, Kevin Gross, Ramon Martinez, Josh Beckett, and a combined no-hitter involving four pitchers in 2018—and the Dodgers' pitching legacy is a rich one.

Perhaps the ballpark's saddest generational moment came with Scully's departure after the 2016 season, making cathedralic Dodger Stadium an unofficial monument to the personable broadcaster, whose voice could for decades be heard echoing within the stadium walls via transistor radios carried by fans, turned to full volume and blaring throughout the confines. Scully, believe those who were reared munching on Dodger Dogs and salted peanuts while listening to him and Doggett announce games, was the face *and* voice of Dodger Stadium beginning the day the ballpark began welcoming fans through its concrete arches and smooth steel turnstiles.

Not only has Dodger Stadium hosted major-league baseball, but numerous other events, some sporting and some not, have been featured there as well. The ballpark served as the 1984 Olympic Games official baseball venue; welcomed Pope John Paul II in 1987; hosted a concert by The Three Tenors, Luciano Pavarotti, Placido Domingo, and Jose Carreras, in 1994; and invited the Beatles to perform [1966] as well as Elvis Presley [1966] and The Jacksons [1984]. Still, baseball continues to prevail. Since it opened, Dodger Stadium has hosted 11 World Series, with the Dodgers winning six of them. The ballpark has also witnessed 15 National League West Division titles and enjoyed a pair of National League wild card winners. Over the six decades that it has welcomed fans, the ballpark has hosted some 4,000 regular-season games. Would the Oakland A's help the Dodgers to a few more World Series victories?

Then-General Manager Fred Claire largely assembled the 1988 Dodgers following the team's pedestrian showing in 1986 and 1987—the club finished 16 games under .500 both years with identical 73-89 records. "Clearly, there was work to be done," said Claire, who had assumed the general manager position on April 6, 1987, and held it for the next 11 years.

"Going into 1988, there were three really glaring needs. One was a shortstop and one was a closer, because we had neither in '86—you can't win without those two positions being filled. The other one was left-handed help in the bullpen. It was a trade at the winter meetings that brought us Alfredo Griffin at shortstop, Jay Howell as the closer, and Jesse Orosco as the left-handed relief pitcher." Also added under Claire's watch were Rick Dempsey, Gibson, and Mike Davis, enabling the club to field a much more formidable squad in 1988. A World Series-caliber team, as it turned out.

Starting for the Dodgers in Game One was a who's who of offensively inconsequential players—literally: anyone perusing their names on a lineup card would likely exclaim, "Who? WHO?"

None were bona fide stars compared with what the A's were serving up. However, all were at least capable ballplayers—capable enough, that is, to start in the first game of the World Series for one of the historically greatest franchises. For most of those players, that capability was largely a defensive one.

"If you looked at the [regular-season] stats, we should have lost," said the late Ben Hines, who was in the first year of his second multi-year stint as the Dodgers' hitting coach. Still, "Based on the fact that Orel [Hershiser] would probably get two wins, and possibly be available for

Kirk Gibson at Michigan State University, circa 1979 (courtesy of Michigan State University Athletic Communications).

long relief in the other [games], then possibly come back around to start Game Seven, I felt we had a good chance."

The starting lineup for Game One, presented to umpires just before the first pitch, was described by NBC broadcaster Bob Costas as possibly the weakest lineup ever fielded in a World Series. Lasorda agreed.

"We had a bunch of nobodies," he said. "Someone said, 'I wouldn't bet a nickel on that team.' We had lost quite a few games during the regular season, and most of the time I was just looking for a base hit."

The Dodgers lineup for Game One included:

Steve Sax, at second base, a career .281 hitter with only 54 lifetime home runs to his credit and a propensity for wildness, particularly when trying to throw runners out at first base. His unsolicited nickname, at least to fans seated in his line of fire above the visitors' dugout—devotees who trembled with consternation every time he threw a ball to first base—was "Steve scatter arm."

Franklin Stubbs, first base, a lifetime .232 hitter who never drove in more than 71 runs in a season. In 10 major-league campaigns, the quiet Stubbs averaged 10 home runs and 34 RBI, modest numbers by any standard but good enough for the 27-year-old North Carolina native, who also played in the outfield, to start for the light-hitting 1988 Dodgers. When he joined the Dodgers, a collective "Who?" was heard resonating across Los Angeles.

Mickey Hatcher, left field, a career .280 player who hit nine home runs in his most successful long-ball season. The popular Hatcher never drove in more than 69 runs in a season, although he was noted for hustling on the base paths and in the field. Hatcher was a catalyst for the team and a prime reason why the ball club performed as well as it did in 1988.

Mike Marshall, right field, who batted cleanup for the Dodgers despite hitting only 20 home runs that season. Marshall, a quiet, unemotional athlete, played 11 seasons in the big leagues and hit 148 home runs, mediocre numbers for a cleanup hitter who was groomed in the farm system and elevated to hit home runs. He hit them, just not as often as expected.

John Shelby, center field, a .239 hitter whose previous high for RBI was 72. Shelby hit .268 in 1988.

Mike Scioscia, catcher, a .259 hitter whose high-water mark for home runs in a single season was 12. Scioscia, who was well-liked by his

Dodgers teammates and later managed the Anaheim and Los Angeles Angels for 19 seasons, hit only .257 with three home runs in 1988.

Jeff Hamilton, third base, a .234 hitter who drove in only 124 runs in a six-year career—an average of just over 20 per season. A more-than-capable defensive third baseman who would be called upon to pitch during a marathon extra-inning game in 1989, Hamilton hit only six home runs in 1988 and was generally regarded as a weak and inconsistent hitter.

Alfredo Griffin, shortstop, who hit just 24 home runs in an 18-year career. Griffin hit a minuscule .199 during the 1988 season and, like Hamilton, was more highly regarded for his fielding than for his performance at the plate. Griffin, in his first and worst season with the club, would hit just .160 in the National League Championship Series and .188 in the World Series.

Tim Belcher, pitcher, a rare rookie making an opening-game start in the World Series. Belcher's lifetime ERA was a mediocre 4.16; his offensive production was limited to only four hits in 1988 and his career batting average over 14 seasons would be an unremarkable .124.[6]

Managing the team was Tommy Lasorda, who was then in his 13th season at the club's helm. Lasorda's best record had been 98-64 in 1977, and he had won National League pennants in 1977 and 1978 and a world championship in 1981.

Perhaps most imposing was the one player who figured not to play that day: the intense and highly talented Gibson, although in 1988 his regular-season statistics lagged far behind other hitters in the National League. On the year Gibson had hit .290 [not in the top 10 and well behind the league leader, Tony Gwynn, who hit .313] with 25 home runs [tied for seventh behind the league leader, Strawberry, who had 39] and only 76 RBI [again not in the top 10, trailing even his teammate Marshall, who had 82]. Although he'd had better seasons offensively, including a high of 91 RBI while with the Detroit Tigers in 1984, Gibson's 1988 numbers would be good enough to earn him the league's top offensive honor: an MVP Award. Most agree the award was presented to Gibson largely due to the intangibles he brought to the team, inspiring them through his leadership to achieve more than their physical capabilities afforded. In short, what the 1988 Dodgers lacked in the hitting department they more than made up for by doing other things, with Gibson setting the example: hustling, stealing bases, sacrificing runners over, moving runners along in other ways, and generally making things happen. As Lasorda noted before the game began, it seemed to him that Gibson was the most valuable player in the National League. Who could argue?

In sharp contrast to the Dodgers' weak lineup, the A's Game One starting lineup was much more formidable, featuring solid hitting and pitching and several leaders in various offensive categories. It included:

> Carney Lansford, at third base, a former batting champion [1981] and all-star who continued on to compile a lifetime .305 batting average in eight postseason series, including three World Series.

> Dave Henderson, center field, who hit 24 home runs, drove in 94 runners, and batted .304 during the 1988 season.

> Jose Canseco, right field, who won two-thirds of a triple crown in 1988. His 42 home runs and 124 RBI led the American League; he would also lead the league in home runs with 44 in 1991 and would ultimately knock 462 balls out of major-league ballparks before retiring in 2001. Canseco, the American League MVP for 1988, would figure prominently both offensively and in the outfield during Game One.

> Dave Parker, left field, a two-time batting champ [1977 and 1978] who led the league in RBI in 1985. Parker had an off year in 1988 with only 12 home runs and 55 RBI, although he would drive in 97 runners the next season. Parker had been named National League MVP a decade earlier.

Mark McGwire, first base, a product of USC coach Rod Dedeaux's major-league preparatory factory. The former American League home run champ [he hit 49 the previous season and would hit 70 and 65 in 1998 and 1999] hit 32 blasts in 1988 and drove in 99 runners. He finished fourth in home runs to teammate Canseco, and the two would become known as the Bash Brothers.

Terry Steinbach, catcher. Although his offensive numbers weren't strong, Steinbach was an all-star in 1988.

Glenn Hubbard, second base, another weak offensive link but a capable fielder. With a lifetime batting average of .244, Hubbard had hit only 57 home runs in 11 previous seasons.

Walt Weiss, shortstop, a second-year player who hit .250 in 1988 with three home runs and 39 RBI.

Dave Stewart, pitcher, a former Dodger, who was ace of the Oakland pitching staff. His 21 wins and 3.32 ERA led the team in both departments, and Stewart had just completed his second of four consecutive seasons winning 20 games or more—he would win 21 games in 1989 and 22 games in 1990. Over those four seasons Stewart would finish among the top four for the Cy Young Award balloting four times. Although he had no opportunity to hit in the American League, he did have a lifetime batting average of just under .200 based upon six seasons hitting in the National League—not a bad statistical achievement for a pitcher.[7]

In his third season with the team and 10th campaign overall, the A's were managed by Tony La Russa. La Russa, who would eventually win three world championships, had not yet won a pennant. He would manage in the big leagues for 36 years, 10 of them with Oakland.

While the lineups were disparate—one team, the A's, had excessive power and the other one, the Dodgers, did not—the managerial matchup was not dissimilar. Both Lasorda, a former short-term Dodger pitcher who played on Brooklyn's 1955 world championship team, and La Russa, who played for the Kansas City and Oakland Athletics in the 1960s and 1970s, were eventually inducted into the National Baseball Hall of Fame, Lasorda with two world championships and La Russa with three. The primary difference between the two men was their longevity, which was significant: La Russa managed various teams for 35 years before stepping down after the 2011 season following 16 consecutive campaigns with the Cardinals, while Lasorda guided the Dodgers for two decades in the 1970s, 1980s, and 1990s before retiring after the 1996 season.

As Game One prepared for flight, Stewart, the veteran pitcher whose vulnerability was occasional wildness, appeared poised and calm. Whether he remained that way as the players took the field and play began largely depended upon his pitching acumen and the Dodgers' light-hitting starting lineup. Light-hitting, perhaps, but not inept. In baseball, where the least likely players can win ballgames at any given moment, anything is possible. Lasorda was hoping his Dodgers, who had already slain one dragon in an unlikely finish, could slay one more.

CHAPTER 2

THE ROOKIE

When the Dodgers made it to the World Series, my dad decided to invite me to accompany him to the game. He thought it would be fun for me, and there was lots of excitement because it was the first game of the World Series.

We sat along the third-base line in the loge seats. They were really good seats. [With the Dodgers losing most of the game,] I personally got a little discouraged—my brothers and my father may have had more faith in the boys in blue than I did. There just didn't seem to be much hope late in the game—nothing was happening. I remember thinking, "Oh, no, it's not going to happen for them this game."

I remember my dad and my brothers talking about whether Kirk Gibson would play. Will they put him in as a pinch hitter? He was supposed to be so good, but he was injured. They had to do something to pull a rabbit out of the hat.

My dad and my brothers knew instantly when he came out, and because they did, I did too. That's when the buzz really started. There was a lot of cheering.

That was the only game I've ever stayed to the end of, and I've gone to Dodger games my whole life. Even though it seemed like a long shot that something might happen, nobody was willing to give up hope.

He limped up there and I remember the crack of the bat. The next thing I knew, he was rounding the bases and pumping his arm. The stands erupted. It was unbelievable—you couldn't hear anything. There was so much screaming and yelling. There were people crying. That went on for a lot longer than it took him to round the bases. I'm glad I stayed—I'm not sure anything tops it. —Careen Jones, 65, Covina, California

With energy, purpose, and a brisk glide that carried him speedily to his slightly elevated position on the field before most of his teammates had reached theirs, perhaps symbolizing his eagerness to take on the challenging task that lay ahead of him, Tim Belcher, whose 27th birthday was just four days away, walked toward the Dodger Stadium pitching mound to start Game One of the 1988 World Series. At 6-feet-3 and 210 pounds Belcher, from Mount Gilead, Ohio, and Sparta High School, was not a small man, and the season and a fraction that he'd spent in the Dodgers organization were hopeful ones: 4-2 with a 2.38 ERA in 34 innings pitched during the 1987 campaign and 12-6 with a 2.91 ERA and 152 strikeouts in 179.2 innings pitched in 1988. Although no longer a first-year player, Belcher was still considered a rookie due to the limited playing time he had seen during the 1987 season, when the team went 73-89 and finished fourth in the National League West Division. As such, he would finish third that year in the Rookie of the Year balloting, behind Cincinnati's Chris Sabo and Chicago's Mark Grace.

Typically, teams pitch their most dominant starter in the first game of a World Series, hoping to claim an early advantage—especially at home, where two wins early on can be difficult for any club to overcome, even a powerhouse like the Oakland A's. However, then-two-time-all-star Orel Hershiser, who was 24-8 with his recent playoff win against the Mets and had thrown a record number of consecutive scoreless innings—equivalent to 6-1/2 consecutive shutouts—toward the end of a magnificent season, had started Game Seven of the National League Championship Series just three days earlier, had thrown a complete game shutout, and was unavailable to start. Tim Leary, who was 17-11 with a 2.91 ERA, had started Game Six the previous day, so four days later the Dodgers elected to go with the youngster Belcher, who was adequately rested and whose 2.91 ERA would be among the best of his 14-year major-league career.

"If a guy can pitch, a guy can pitch," said Ricky Horton, a relief pitcher on the 1988 Dodgers squad. "Young or old, it just doesn't make any difference. Tim Belcher was not the kind of guy who got scared, so nobody was too worried about him. He wasn't mentally brittle at all—he was certainly up to the task."

When his first pitch sailed toward leadoff hitter Carney Lansford it would mark only the ninth time since 1903, when the first World Series was held, that a rookie had started Game One. An inning later, when the Oakland A's nearly broke the game open with their patented power platoon, the pressure may have leaked.

The first inning was a different story altogether, although Lansford, a first-ball, fastball hitter who walked only 35 times during the regular season, was anything but a certain out—that's why manager Tony La Russa had him batting in the leadoff spot. Hitting .279 on the regular season, with seven home runs and 57 RBI, Lansford was an aggressive hitter and anything but a sure thing to let the first pitch go by in the first game of any series, let alone the World Series. The right-hander Belcher wound up and drilled a fastball down the middle that Lansford watched sail by him and into the glove of catcher Mike Scioscia—thump!—for a called first strike. Just like that the first game of the 1988 World Series, now referred to by fans everywhere as the Kirk Gibson Game even though the Dodgers' star outfielder was at that point already undergoing treatment at the hands of trainers inside the Dodgers clubhouse, was under way.

As Lansford stood focused in the batter's box, waiting for Belcher's next delivery, a pair of former Dodgers representatives looked on from key vantage points near the rust-colored brick infield. Rene Lachemann, the A's trusted first-base coach who four years earlier had managed the Milwaukee Brewers, had been a ballboy for the Dodgers when Dodger Stadium first opened in 1962; later on the Dodgers' current batboy, a former junior college pitcher named Mitch Poole, would play a prominent role in helping to determine the outcome of Game One. Across the diamond stood feisty Jim Lefebvre, the A's third-base coach and Rookie of the Year for the Dodgers in 1965; Lefebvre was a member of the winning World Series team his rookie season and played for the Dodgers in a losing World Series effort the following year, 1966, his sophomore season with the ball club. On that day the allegiance to Oakland of both Lachemann and Lefebvre was a lock as both attempted to lead their team past the organization that gave them their start.

"We felt we were a better team than the Dodgers going into that series," said Lachemann, who later managed four big-league teams. "We had more talent on our club. We felt our lineup was better than theirs.

"For me, it was a big deal to get back to Dodger Stadium because I had been a ballboy there in 1962. Coming back and being in the World Series was something very special to me."

With the count to Lansford 0-1, Belcher, who had an acceptable curveball, came back with six consecutive fastballs—three of them balls and three of them strikes, including two that Lansford hit foul. In a pitch that could have figured prominently as the inning progressed, the final fastball that umpire Doug Harvey called for a third strike to send Lansford back to the dugout appeared to miss the strike zone.

"Obviously, I felt it was not a strike because I took the pitch," Lansford said. "Umpires are human. [Harvey] thought it was a strike, and that's the way it went. [A walk] could've [changed the tenor of the game]."

Of those first pitches in the 1988 World Series—he would make 29 in the first inning, 71 in all, and a whopping 119 in a Game Four victory that brought the Dodgers to the brink of a championship—Belcher would tell a reporter 25 years later exactly what starting for the Dodgers in that first game, playing for a winning team in the World Series, and participating in the 1988 season in its totality meant to him. The Series, he has come to believe, was a watershed moment in what ultimately evolved into an outstanding baseball career, one that lasted almost a decade and a half and resulted in a more-than-respectable 146 wins and more than 1,500 strikeouts. "I think [the 1988 season] made my career," Belcher said. "I was becoming, in a lot of people's eyes, more of a suspect than a prospect. And to be a key member of a world's championship team in '88, rookie pitcher of the year and everything . . . Had that move never happened or had we never won, or had I never been an integral part of the winning, I think my career would've been quite a bit different."[1]

Timothy Wayne Belcher was born October 19, 1961, in Mount Gilead, Morrow County, Central Ohio. He attended Highland High School in Sparta, then played intercollegiate baseball at Mount Vernon Nazarene University in Mount Vernon, Ohio, a liberal arts college with a Christian foundation and a fundamentalist bent. In 1983, at the age of 22, Belcher was drafted as the first pick in the first round of the Major-League Baseball June amateur draft by the Minnesota Twins. He elected not to sign with the club and the following year was again drafted first in the initial round, this time by the New York Yankees in the secondary phase of the January draft. After later being acquired, ironically, by the Oakland A's in a trade involving Honeycutt, Belcher—the proverbial player to be named later in the deal—was on his way to thespian-like fame, an abundance of good fortune, and eventually a World Series ring.

Belcher signed with the A's and split his first season of professional ball between the Class A Madison Muskies and the Class AA Albany-Colonie A's, winning 12 games overall and losing eight with a 3.49 ERA. During the next two seasons, 1985 and 1986, Belcher competed for the Class AA Huntsville Stars, recording 13 wins and 15 losses. Despite the losing record, he was elevated to the Class AAA Tacoma Tigers for the 1987 season, winning nine games and losing 11, then was sent to the Dodgers in a trade Claire orchestrated as the minor-league campaign wound to a close and major-league clubs began calling up players for either a final look before the long season ended or to help them make a last-minute run for a playoff spot. The Dodgers, who at that point in the season were a longshot to earn a playoff berth, called Belcher up to the big club on August 29, 1987, and he made his major-league debut a week later on September 6, pitching the entire final month of the season and going 4-2 with a 2.38 ERA. The Dodgers liked what they saw.

The next season, 1988, was the versatile Belcher's coming-out year. He made 17 starts for the Dodgers, appeared nine times in relief, earned four saves on top of 12 wins, and was named *Sporting News* Rookie Pitcher of the Year. During the National League Championship Series, Belcher won both games that he started, Games Two and Four, striking

Mount Vernon Nazarene University baseball team photo shows Tim Belcher standing, fifth from left, circa 1982 (courtesy of Mount Vernon Nazarene University).

out 16 batters in 15-1/3 innings. His performances were instrumental in helping to propel the Dodgers to their first World Series appearance in seven years.

"Tim Belcher was a tremendous force," Claire said. "He was an incredible part of our team in '88 and just as solid as he could be."

Although Belcher's stay with the Dodgers was a relatively short one—his final year with the club was 1991 before he moved on to the Cincinnati Reds—he did complete 10 games in 1989 and 42 in his major-league career. Nowadays, most pitchers go an entire season—if not an entire career—without throwing a complete game.

After his years in Los Angeles had concluded, Belcher, a no-nonsense hurler cut from the Don Drysdale mold, moved from team to team, pitching for the Cincinnati Reds, Chicago White Sox, Detroit Tigers, Seattle Mariners, Kansas City Royals, and Anaheim Angels before retiring after the 2000 season with 394 total appearances, four postseason wins, and even two home runs to his credit—one of them coming in 1988.

Although Belcher's career was largely completed without controversy, there was a moment in 1999 that he'd likely rather forget. Pitching against his old team, the Dodgers, Belcher fielded a bunt down the first-base line by the opposing pitcher, Chan Ho Park, and applied a bare-ball tag to Park's chest. He then held Park and appeared to guide him out of the base path. Words were exchanged between the two players, then Park, a native of Korea, suddenly struck Belcher in the face with his elbow and threw a flying kick before the two began rolling around on the infield—surrounded by players who had left their respective dugouts in the event that they'd need to defend their teammate. The only help their teammates needed was assistance keeping the two of them separated. When the dust had cleared, Park was ejected and ultimately suspended for a week while the former Dodger Belcher remained in the game.

Despite his success as a pitcher, Belcher never appeared in an all-star game. However, in 1989, the season after his National League Championship Series and World Series appearances boosted him to prominence, Belcher finished sixth to relief pitcher Mark Davis of the San Diego Padres in the balloting for the National League's Cy Young Award, given annually to the best pitcher in the league. Belcher, with 15 wins and a 2.82 ERA, was arguably one of the best.

The seventh fastball that Belcher delivered to Lansford, the one that appeared to miss the outside corner by a mere fraction of an inch but that umpire Harvey called a third strike, was among the most significant pitches that anyone would throw all day, the exception being a slider that Eckersley would throw to Gibson in the ninth inning. Whether Belcher walked the first batter up in the game or struck him out seemed of little consequence at the time, as there were still 8-1/3 innings of baseball to be played while both teams continued to shake the butterflies out of their respective stomachs. Nothing in the box score of that first game indicates anything other than the fact that Lansford struck out to start the game. But the strikeout, coming on a pitch that registered 95 mph on the radar speed gun, was a significant one if only in retrospect and only after the energy of Game One had begun to subside some three hours after the contest began. More on that later.

With one out and the crowd still getting situated in their brightly colored seats, the next batter up for Oakland was Dave Henderson, another first-ball hitter looking to get something started for his fourth team. Henderson, who was completing his eighth season in the big leagues, was a long-ball threat, hitting at a .304 clip on the season with 24 home runs and 94 RBI. After fouling off a pitch, then watching as a ball outside the strike zone zoomed by to even the count at 1-1, Henderson bounced what's known as a "seeing eye" single through the middle of the infield and on into center field. By the end of the Series, Henderson would record two doubles and three more singles in 20 at-bats, making him one of Oakland's most productive hitters—and one of its *few* productive hitters—at .300; only the catcher Steinbach, who went 4 for 11 in the Series and hit .364, would fare better among the Oakland players [not counting part-timer Stan Javier who, at 2 for 4, batted .500]. At the time, only one thing mattered: Oakland had its first man on base with the always-dangerous Jose Canseco coming to the plate and aging slugger Dave Parker waiting patiently on deck.

Canseco, a low-ball hitter, had amazed onlookers in batting practice the previous day when he blasted a pitch out of Dodger Stadium, something only four players have done during a regular game in the park's 59-year history: former MVPs Giancarlo Stanton and Willie Stargell and 12-time all-stars Mark McGwire and Mike Piazza, the latter a former Dodger and member of the Hall of Fame. Those who witnessed it estimated that Canseco's shot flew a whopping 560 feet from home plate and well over the outfield pavilion, while the longest ball ever hit out of Dodger Stadium during a game traveled a "mere" 506 feet. Had it occurred during a regular-season game, Canseco's batting practice swing would have produced the longest home run ever hit out of the ballpark. Fortunately for the Dodgers . . . it didn't. Still, Canseco was hopeful of replicating the feat in Game One.

The Dodgers' strategy against Canseco, whose bat speed struck terror in the hearts of pitchers, was a simple one: pitch him inside on the hands, where they figured he was unlikely to transfer his full weight and power into a pitch and hit it bouncing through traffic onto the Pasadena Freeway. In that regard, Belcher's first pitch was right where the scouting reports suggested it be, and Canseco took a hard swing at a fastball and

Tim Belcher pitches for Mount Vernon Nazarene University, circa 1982 (courtesy of Mount Vernon Nazarene University).

missed—0-1. Belcher's second pitch was not so well placed, as it trailed in and bounced off Canseco's right forearm. The slugger grimaced, shook the arm repeatedly as if to wobble away the throbbing pain, circled behind the home plate umpire, glanced a couple of times out toward Belcher as if to wonder why he had hit him, then trotted off to first base as Dodgers manager Tommy Lasorda, chomping on a stick of gum, ran out onto the field to plaintively argue that the ball had hit Canseco's bat rather than his prized forearm. Harvey would have none of the veteran manager's argument, which he had tested on umpires many times before, and he was not about to change his ruling based upon the volatile skipper's hope or conjecture. He waved for Canseco to take first base.

Henderson, meanwhile, scrambled off to second and the A's had their first threat of the afternoon in only the first inning. Just like that, the strikeout to Lansford and morphed into something ominous, two runners on base, with the number four hitter Dave Parker, a bit of an anomaly as a cleanup hitter with just 12 home runs and 55 RBI to his credit, walking to the plate. Moments earlier, with Lansford at the plate, Belcher had appeared to be in full control, however it now seemed he was on the ropes. Belcher was in trouble as Parker stepped in for the hoped-for knockout en route to an eventual Game One win.

Hitting coach Hines wasn't worried, not yet. "Belcher got in an out of trouble a lot," he said.

As the 37-year-old Parker stood at home plate, perhaps wondering if this would be his final World Series—it wouldn't, there would be one more the following season—he had completed 16 seasons in the major leagues and recorded 285 home runs, his big season occurring in 1985 when he blasted 34 home runs and notched a National League-leading 125 RBI and 42 doubles for the Pittsburgh Pirates. Although Parker's career was winding down, he remained an at-times potent hitter who could still connect with power and had pedigree credentials: he had won league MVP honors a decade earlier, had finished second or third in the MVP balloting on three other occasions, earned back-to-back batting titles in 1977 and 1978, and was also a seven-time all-star. Still, his home run output had sagged in 1988 and some may have wondered why he was batting cleanup at all with the up-and-coming slugger McGwire, a potential Hall of Famer, batting fifth.

The scouting report on Parker, who throughout his career had been a dangerous hitter with runners on first base, was similar to that for Canseco: pitch him up and in, jam him with an average or better fastball, avoid pitching him low, and keep the speed up on pitches. Belcher had seen the report and would do his best to follow it, although little that Belcher tried to do that day registered much success.

Parker took the first pitch from the big right-hander for a ball, then fouled two off. A ball outside brought the count to 2-2 before Parker fouled off another pitch. Finally, with the count still 2-2, he hit a shallow fly ball to the center fielder Shelby, who recorded the second out with little effort. Theoretically, Belcher was breathing a little easier at that point, although not much easier with McGwire coming to the plate and his Oakland teammates standing on first and second.

Like the aging Parker, the youthful, third-year player McGwire was already a prodigious home run hitter and someone who would be considered increasingly dangerous as his career progressed. With 84 home runs on his resume, more than half of them coming in 1987 [49], there would be 499 more dingers before McGwire would call it quits, retiring after the 2001 season at the age of 38 and on the heels of hitting 29 home runs in his final year of baseball—just two seasons after hitting 65 home runs to once again lead the league [he had led the league the previous season with 70].

Belcher's first two pitches to McGwire, a low-ball hitter and a member of the 1984 U.S. Olympic baseball team, were fouled away. Back came Belcher with three consecutive balls up high and the count was 3-2. Finally, Belcher, who didn't want much to do with McGwire anyway and was pitching him carefully, walked the strapping first baseman to load the bases, bringing Terry Steinbach, a high fastball hitter, to the plate. A fair home run threat who would belt 162 over major-league fences during his productive career, Steinbach had homered off Mets ace Dwight Gooden in the all-star game earlier in the season.

Belcher fell behind Steinbach early on with a low curveball and a low fastball before the 26-year-old former ninth-round draft pick hit a lazy fly ball to left-center field on Belcher's 29th pitch of the inning. Shelby caught the ball running in for his second putout of the inning and the threat was extinguished. Oakland had brought six men to the plate and stranded three of them.

Looking back to a point earlier in the inning, Belcher was probably counting his blessings that home plate umpire Harvey had called a third strike on a full-count pitch to Lansford that appeared to be out of the strike zone. Had Belcher walked Lansford, then followed with the hit by Parker, Canseco's free pass resulting from the pitched ball that struck his arm, and McGwire's walk, the entire dynamic of the inning might have changed. At the very least, Oakland would have taken an early 1-0 lead, the Dodgers would have been put on the defensive, and the team's entire strategy for the rest of the game might well have changed.

Instead, Belcher was out of the inning, although not without some wear and tear. Whether he was ineffective in the inning or just pitching carefully to Oakland's top hitters was uncertain. He had thrown nearly 30 pitches after just half an inning and the likelihood that he would make it past the third or fourth inning if everything from there on out went perfectly was questionable. Belcher clearly needed to pull his game together as he prepared to face the bottom three batters in the Oakland lineup the following inning. As Oakland took the field for the first time in the Series, the Dodgers had some fireworks of their own in store.

CHAPTER 3

THE VETERAN

My seats for Game One were part of the season tickets we received at the company I was running, so I chose to attend the first game. We had four tickets in the loge section of the stadium above the field boxes, great seats. I took three of my four children. The Dodgers were not expected to win the Series—Oakland was definitely favored. When it got to the ninth inning, Oakland had their star pitcher, Dennis Eckersley, in the game. When Kirk Gibson came up his home run was just about in a direct line with where we were seated—we were looking straight ahead as the ball went out over the right-field fence and into the bleachers. We had a perfect view of it. It was the most exciting single event that I ever saw—it still stands out in my memory. I've seen a couple of no-hitters. I've seen pitchers like Koufax strike out 16 or 18 in a game. I've seen a lot of interesting events, but the Kirk Gibson homer by far is the standout.

No one had seen Gibson in the dugout, as he was injured, and during the ninth inning he walked out of the dugout and the crowd went wild. He'd been the guy carrying the team with his hitting throughout the year. The Dodgers had a man on base with a walk, and the crowd really responded to Gibson coming to bat. He could barely walk, so we didn't know how he was going to do. When he hit the home run, the crowd went nuts—I've never been to a place where the ovation was as loud or as long. They must have applauded and yelled and screamed for 20 minutes straight. There was an electric feeling in the crowd, and it is impossible to recapture that.

We ducked out and got started for our car after 20 minutes or more. There was still lots of cheering going on, and very few people were moving toward their vehicles. The Dodgers were so energized by that Kirk Gibson hit that they went on and won the Series—that home run in the first game was a watershed event. Looking back, the Dodgers hung in there, but I don't recall much of the game before the ninth inning.

My pattern through the years had been to leave the games in the seventh or eighth inning to get a jump on the traffic, but for some reason we had no intention of leaving early that night—it was a World Series game and we were there to the very end. [With all the cheering that continued inside the stadium] we beat the crowd anyway. —Glade Merkley, who died in 2020 at the age of 88.

It is generally acknowledged that good pitching trumps good hitting. There are, of course, exceptions—outstanding hitters occasionally overcome pitching excellence even when their teammates fail to hit, but most of the time a great pitcher who is on his game is virtually unstoppable. Because of that, and because he was often unstoppable himself, the eyes of his teammates were all on the 6-foot-2, 200-pound, 31-year-old Dave Stewart, a native of Oakland who had spent four reasonably impressive seasons or portions thereof—1978, 1981, 1982, and 1983—with the Dodgers early on in his career, winning 18 games, losing 13, and earning seven saves as a member of the team's vaunted bullpen. His ERA during those years was 0.00 in one appearance during the 1978 season, then 2.49 in 1981, 3.81 in 1982, and 2.96 in 1983.

Still, after compiling a 5-2 record during the first half of the 1983 season, Stewart was sent packing to the Texas Rangers for three seasons [1983-85] and the Philadelphia Phillies for two more after that [1985-86] before finally settling in with his hometown team: the once-gimmicky Oakland A's, whose white shoes and green and yellow uniforms screamed for attention. His career record upon joining the A's was an inauspicious 40-45 and Stewart had demonstrated a tendency to record high ERAs, at least in the early years of his career: 5.46 in 1985 and 6.23

and 6.57 during his final two seasons in Philadelphia. Then, something clicked for the big right-hander, a 16th-round draft pick in 1975 out of St. Elizabeth's High School in Oakland. During his first season with the A's, Stewart finished 9-5 with a 3.74 ERA and 102 strikeouts in 149.1 innings pitched, giving him a measure of optimism that a brighter baseball future lay ahead of him. With his confidence unabated, Stewart went 20-13 with a 3.68 ERA the following season, 1987, with 205 strikeouts in 261.1 innings pitched, and 21-12 with a 3.23 ERA and 192 strikeouts in 275.2 innings pitched in the pennant-winning 1988 campaign. In only three seasons, Stewart became a workhorse for the team, and the work was usually good. Good enough to lead his team to the World Series in 1988, something the Athletics would also accomplish in 1989 [they would win the Series that year and Stewart would be named World Series MVP after compiling an impressive 2-0 record with a 1.69 ERA] and 1990, when they lost in disquieting fashion.

"Dave Stewart was a talented pitcher," Claire said. "The Dodgers lost Dave [in 1983], but knowing him and what a good person he is, it was great to see how he came back as a player and how he has done so well in his post-player career. He's really just a very good person."

After graduating from St. Elizabeth's, Stewart was selected 24th by the Dodgers in the 16th round of major-league baseball's 1975 June amateur draft, electing, like many young ballplayers who are confident of their ability, to play minor-league ball rather than attend college. He broke in with the Bellingham Dodgers in low Class A ball, eventually moving to the Danville Dodgers, again in Class A, was shifted back to Bellingham, was sent up to the Albuquerque Dodgers in Class AAA, then dropped back down to the Clinton Dodgers in Class A where he compiled a 17-4 record. He was elevated to the Dodgers' major-league club in 1978 for two innings in a single game, then retreated to the San Antonio Dodgers in Class AA in 1978 and was again elevated back up to Albuquerque in 1979 and 1980 before once again joining the Dodgers and remaining at the big-league level for the remainder of his baseball career. Stewart's minor-league resume noted a 69-46 record with a respectable 4.00 ERA and 610 strikeouts in 859 innings pitched. At the Class AAA level, he was 27-22 with a satisfactory 4.37 ERA, satisfactory considering that minor-league travel could be exhausting. Not every ballpark he visited was constructed to bring out the best in pitchers.

Stewart succeeded in carving out an outstanding major-league career, although it took him seven seasons at various levels of minor-league baseball to finally achieve his dream. His best season at any level was in 1990 with the Oakland A's, going 22-11 with a 2.56 ERA. That was the season when the A's were swept in the World Series by the Cincinnati Reds, four games to none. There would be only one more World Series for Stewart after that one, in 1993, when the Toronto Blue Jays, his last club before rejoining the A's for a final major-league season, beat his former club, the Philadelphia Phillies, 4-2.

"Stewart was a heckuva pitcher—he had good stuff, he had great command of his pitches, and he knew what he was doing with the ball," said Dodgers third-base coach Joe Amalfitano, who joined the team as coach in 1983—Stewart's last season with the club. "He was one of [Oakland's] best starters—probably number one. When you get to [the World Series], you're going to pitch the best."

Like knights heading out to wage war, the Los Angeles Dodgers trotted confidently onto the field at Dodger Stadium to begin battling the A's in the first inning of Game One. Rick Honeycutt, the Dodger pitching coach from 2006 through 2019, played for the A's and the Dodgers in 1987 and pitched effectively for Oakland during the 1988 World Series. He recalled the team's attitude heading into that confrontation.

"We were confident, but not overconfident," Honeycutt said, matter-of-factly.

Finally, after 168 games for the Dodgers, including seven playoff games, and 166 for the A's over the previous 6-1/2 months, the table was set for two: two teams and roughly 50 players. Included were a premiere American League pitcher [Stewart] and a premier National League pitcher [Hershiser]; two of baseball's most prolific single-season home run hitters [McGwire and his compatriot slugger Canseco]; a self-confident right fielder who would figure prominently in Andy Pafko-esque fashion [again Canseco]; two future Hall of Fame-caliber managers [Lasorda and

La Russa]; and a Hall of Fame broadcaster [Scully]. Each would preside over the greatest spectacle in baseball and perhaps all of sports: the World Series. Some believed the game might evolve into a laugher, with Oakland starting a massacre of the weak-hitting Dodgers on their home turf. Others, having watched the Dodgers scrap and claw their way to victory over come-from-behind victory all season long—91 wins in all against 70 losses—knew better. Both teams had come to play at the highest possible level, and although Oakland had hit the bullseye by achieving the coveted 100 win mark against just 62 losses, each team badly wanted to win this California Series and the bragging rights that accompanied it. Oakland appeared to have a big edge, at least based upon statistics, but so did the Mets in their National League Championship Series against the Dodgers, which had ended just days earlier with the Dodgers in the driver's seat and winning in seven games. In the end it was the Hershiser-led Dodgers, aided by Gibson's two home runs and six RBI but only four hits overall, that made the difference in that series. In contrast, the A's, led by Canseco's three home runs, four RBI, and .313 batting average, had dismantled the Boston Red Sox, sweeping them in four games on the strength of seven home runs, a team batting average of nearly .300, and a staff ERA of just 2.00. Heading down to Los Angeles, the A's had won five consecutive games and were rested and confident while the Dodgers were slightly weary, perhaps less confident, and unequivocally overmatched. For Oakland, what could possibly go wrong?

CHAPTER 4

FIRST BLOOD – 2-0

My brother and I were outside playing, and our mom came and told us that Uncle John was on the phone and he wanted to talk with me. As I picked up the phone he said, "What are you doing tonight?" I told him I was going to watch the Dodger game [on television]. He asked me if I wanted to GO to the Dodger game, and I said: "Of course!"

We arrived at Dodger Stadium so early that the parking lot gates weren't even open yet. We parked down the hill and walked to the stadium, which was still pretty empty because we were among the first ones there. We watched the Dodgers and the A's take batting practice—Canseco and McGwire were hitting balls out of the park. I bought a program and a hat, and I still have my ticket stub—autographed by Kirk Gibson. We sat in loge section 145.

I was 11, and since the Dodgers had just beaten the Mets I thought no one could beat them—I believed it was the Dodgers' year. The A's had a powerful team, but the Dodgers seemed to have good chemistry and team spirit. Gibson had changed that team—I thought, "This team is different."

When Canseco hit the grand slam the ball hit a camera in center field. I remember thinking, "Wow!" But, there was still a feeling in the stadium that something magical was going to happen—we were confident the whole game. We never left the games early—baseball is one of those sports where you don't leave early.

We were sitting five or six rows behind third base so that we couldn't see into the Dodger dugout. When we saw that number 23 come out of the dugout, there was suddenly this hope within the crowd. I thought, "It's Gibson!" I was just a kid, and I was standing on my seat. The home run seemed like slow motion and the stadium shook like an earthquake—I've never felt Dodger Stadium shake that way. We couldn't stop cheering him, and we stayed in the stadium for another 15 or 20 minutes.

After Game One, I think all Dodger fans knew that we'd just won the World Series. —Jason Arellano, 44, Alta Loma, California

---

While the A's had squandered their initial scoring opportunity, the Dodgers had little notion of replicating that failure. Players knew they were overmatched, at least offensively. They understood that they would have to capitalize on every potential scoring opportunity that came their way if they had any hope of winning the World Series. It wouldn't take long for one of those opportunities to come along, and the man who would instigate it had been a mastermind of rallies all season long: the caffeinated Mickey Hatcher. Hatcher wasted little time helping his team overcome a pitching matchup that seemed to some more like a pitching mismatch.

"It probably was," Oakland relief pitcher Greg Cadaret said of the Belcher vs. Stewart duel.

In the first inning, leading off for the Dodgers was second baseman Steve Sax, who had played briefly in the 1981 World Series that the Dodgers won in six games. A rookie during his first Series, Sax's contribution to the world championship had been minimal: he played in just two games, going 0 for 1.

Facing Sax on this day was forkball thrower Dave Stewart, a teammate of his on that 1981 world championship team. Stewart wasted no time demonstrating to his former teammate that there was no place for sentimentality in the World Series, his first pitch hitting Sax behind the left shoulder and sending him sprawling onto the dirt around home

Dave Stewart (National Baseball Hall of Fame.)

plate. Undaunted, Sax sprang to his feet and sprinted off toward first base like a man on fire while the umpire Harvey, eager to avoid a bench-clearing scrum and suspecting that Stewart might have been trying to retaliate after Belcher plunked Canseco earlier in the inning, warned the pitcher that any further shenanigans, either perceived or real, would be cause for ejection. The Dodgers' GM Claire dismissed the notion that Belcher hitting Canseco and Stewart plunking Sax represented anything more than World Series intensity run slightly amok.

"It was just the game," Claire said. "Those don't stand out in my memory because there was no major turmoil—no fight, no suspension, or anything else that resulted. That's the way the game is played. There wasn't anything that stood out"—not even some much-publicized bickering that occurred between Baylor and Howell before the Series began. More on that later.

Second up for the Dodgers was Franklin Stubbs, who battled Stewart for several minutes before hitting a fly ball to the center fielder Henderson moments after drilling a ball just foul down the right-field line that nearly hit the first-base umpire Durwood Merrill and might have gone for extra bases if its trajectory had been mere inches to the left. That brought the left fielder Hatcher, a contact hitter with little power, up to face Stewart.

On May 15, 1955, Michael Vaughn Hatcher, nicknamed Mickey, was born in Cleveland, Ohio, near Lake Erie. After moving to Arizona he eventually graduated from Mesa High School near Phoenix, becoming a two-sport standout—baseball and football—as a prep schooler. After attending nearby Mesa Community College for two years, where he became an all-American in both sports, Hatcher enrolled at the University of Oklahoma, an athletics powerhouse where he excelled at baseball and football, the latter sport as a wide receiver under legendary coach Barry Switzer. While playing for Switzer, Hatcher caught two passes in the 1976 Fiesta Bowl, which the Sooners won, 41-7. With the two catches—Oklahoma only threw for 23 yards in the entire game—Hatcher became the team's leading pass receiver that day on his home turf in Tempe, Arizona.

"I did all right at football," Hatcher said, adding that, "Baseball was the sport I felt like I had to keep playing. One of the reasons I went to junior college was to play both sports. When I was All-American in both sports, I wanted to keep playing."[1] He did just that, for the next 19 seasons both collegiately and professionally.

During and after college, Hatcher was drafted three times by major-league baseball organizations: by the Houston Astros in the 14th round of the 1974 Major-League Baseball June amateur draft [the 327th pick overall], by the New York Mets in the second round of the 1976 January draft-regular phase [the 38th selection overall], and by the Dodgers in the fifth round of the 1977 June amateur draft [number 124 overall].

"I got drafted [by the Dodgers] as an outfielder," Hatcher said. "They had no third basemen in the organization, and at that time I was swinging the bat pretty well. They asked me if I'd try third base. It got me through the organization fast."[2]

With such impressive versatility, it quickly became apparent that Hatcher's future, at least his near future, was with the Dodgers organization, although a long hiatus would ensue after his first two seasons with the club and a subsequent trade to the Minnesota Twins before he returned to Los Angeles as a free agent.

After signing with the Dodgers, Hatcher reported to the team's Class A affiliate, the Clinton Dodgers, in 1977, but he didn't stay long. He slugged 11 home runs, driving in 53 runners and hitting .309, opening the eyes of management and earning a promotion to Class AA San Antonio and later Class AAA Albuquerque the following season. At both venues his home run totals sagged. However, his batting average didn't and he hit .332 in San Antonio and .329 in Albuquerque. Already, his ability to bang out hits and drive in runs—he has been called the "poster boy for contact hitting"[3] and a scrapper—was becoming his preferred style of play, and the parent Dodgers were undoubtedly thrilled.

A second season in Albuquerque, 1979, where he hit .371 on the strength of 10 home runs and 93 RBI, was all the team needed to see, and Hatcher made his major-league debut later that season. Although he saw limited action with just 93 at-bats, he still managed to hit four doubles, a triple, and a home run while logging a respectable .269 batting average for the club.

Despite that success, the 1980 season found him back in Albuquerque, where his numbers were once again impressive: seven home runs, 40 RBI, and a .359 batting average. He was inexplicably traded to the Minnesota Twins.

After that, Hatcher would not return to the minors, spending the 1981-1986 seasons with the Twins and playing numerous positions: first base, third base, left field, right field, and center field. Perhaps more importantly, his reputation as a jack of all trades had been firmly established in the eyes of anyone watching.

The Dodgers were watching. After the 1987 season, and just in time to play in the World Series the following year, Hatcher was returned to the Dodgers in Claire's first transaction just days after taking over as general manager. At the same time, the club released pitcher Jerry Reuss and swallowed the remainder of the pitcher's $1.35 million contract. It was a potentially expensive gamble, but one that ultimately paid big rewards for the Dodgers as they attempted to climb back into the World Series.

"He'll be a good swing man for us," manager Lasorda said at the time. "A position like that, it takes an experienced guy to do that."[4]

Hatcher *was* experienced, and Lasorda's confidence was not misplaced. Playing first base, third base, and the outfield for the Dodgers, Hatcher hit seven home runs, drove in 42 runners, and batted .282; he flirted with .300 the following season, eventually finishing at .293. While the home runs had diminished in number, Hatcher had found a role as playmaker for one of the best teams in baseball.

When asked once about his ability to hit home runs and his inclination, if there was one, to majestically circle the bases afterward, Hatcher replied matter-of-factly. "I do not practice the home run trot," he said. "I do not have a home run trot. I don't have any experience at it."[5]

Those watching the 1988 World Series would take a different view of Hatcher as a home run hitter once the energy from those five games had subsided. In the first inning of Game One, the energy was just beginning to click.

"Mickey was someone who I've [mentioned] a lot in terms of what we liked in the makeup, dedication, and determination of a player," Claire said. "Mickey had all of those things. He loved to play the game and his teammates loved him."

Amalfitano described Hatcher as a team catalyst. "He was a big part of our success, not just in that World Series but in our season. He had a lot of big hits. In the World Series he also contributed very well."

As he usually did, especially during the long 1988 season when his hustle became a trademark characteristic among loyal followers in Los Angeles, Hatcher entered the right side of the batter's box with obvious deliberation, his short, quick steps indicative of a ballplayer on a mission.

All season long, Hatcher appeared to be on a mission, and the effort was often reflected in the dirt that his uniform collected during most games. Hall of Famer Mike Schmidt once said that "If you could equate the amount of time and effort put in mentally and physically into succeeding on the baseball field and measured it by the dirt on your uniform, mine would have been black."[6] Hatcher's uniform might have been blacker.

The right-hander Stewart toed the pitching rubber, stared down toward the catcher Steinbach for signs, and wound up to deliver his first pitch to the right-handed Hatcher, who after a couple of practice swings bent slightly at the waist in anticipation of the pitch. Stewart then sent a fastball zipping toward the outside corner of the plate and into Steinbach's mitt for what appeared to be a called first strike. In an instant, however, the third-base umpire, Derryl Cousins, discounted the strike, instead calling a balk—Stewart had committed 16 balks and 14 wild pitches during the regular season—and Sax was afforded the free base as the umpires waved him over to second. Meanwhile, Steinbach trotted out to the mound in an obligatory effort to settle his pitcher down while Hatcher looked on from a spot just outside the batter's box. In their first at-bat with just one away, the underdog Dodgers already had a man in scoring position.

Hatcher stepped back between the chalk lines, crouched again at the plate, and stared out toward Stewart, who appeared to be either flustered or nervous just moments into the first inning. On the next pitch Stewart came back with another fastball that Hatcher fouled back against the blue trim beneath the backstop screen, putting the pitcher ahead of the count as the ball bounced and spun toward the first-base side and the A's dugout, where hope at that moment sprang eternal.

With the count then 0-1, Stewart delivered another fastball that Hatcher, known throughout the league as a contact hitter, was expecting. He drilled it solidly toward the left-field fence on a line drive. As the outfielder Parker retreated onto the warning track in an effort to put his glove on the ball, it drifted over his head, sailed over the sky blue fence, and hit a rail between the 370- and 385-feet mark, bouncing back onto the playing field as the boisterous Dodger Stadium crowd erupted in a crescendo of cheers. Hatcher sprinted around the bases in his classic style of hustle, clenching his fists above his shoulders as he rounded second base with manager Lasorda applauding from the dugout.

"When you consider that he only hit one home run all season long, then he hit one in his first at-bat in the World Series, something was in our favor," hitting coach Hines reflected.

Hatcher was greeted at home plate by his teammate Sax, who had scored along with Hatcher on the home run, and then sprinted toward the Dodger dugout, elation written on his face. The sprint didn't go unnoticed by at least one Southern California sportswriter, *LA Times* columnist Ostler, who wondered publicly before Game One of the World Series, "How can [the Dodgers] possibly top their 4-games-to-3 win over the Mets in the series to end all series?" Soon enough, Ostler would have his answer, as would all of Southern California and 50,000 screaming Game One spectators.

"He runs to first on walks," Ostler wrote, describing Hatcher's heart for the game and his baseball soul. "He runs to first and then back to the dugout on groundouts. Mickey is the only guy in the big leagues who would run out a strikeout—if he ever struck out, which he didn't in [the NLCS series against the Mets]."

Continued Ostler: "In this age of blasé athletes, Hatcher runs around the ballpark like a rookie batboy. This was Mr. Electricity of the [Mets] series. The fans couldn't wait to see where Mickey would hit his next double or how close he would come to killing himself chasing a foul popup. The Dodgers didn't win a game without a significant contribution from Hatcher, the 33-year-old retread who had been waived out of the game when the Dodges picked him up last season."[7]

Fast forward a few games and Hatcher was still at it, hustling around the bases when a simple home run trot would have sufficed. He was all emotion, with a jigger of adrenaline added to the baseball cocktail for good measure. When Hatcher cleared the base paths, by whatever means—double, triple, home run—it took a little longer for the dust stirred by his cleats to settle onto the ground.

Mickey Hatcher, Oklahoma University, 1977 (courtesy of Oklahoma University).

After his first-inning home run against the A's, Hatcher was greeted by a wave of teammates. Just like that, the Dodgers led Game One and the 84th World Series [technically, 1988 marked the 86th World Series. However, the 1904 Series was canceled when the New York Giants refused to play the champions of what they claimed as an inferior league; the 1994 Series was canceled due to a players strike], 2-0.

The home run should not have surprised anyone. Hatcher had been a catalyst for the team all year long. Although he hit only one home run during the entire regular season, driving in 25 runners, he did have a career-best nine home runs in 1983, and before Game One had hit 36 homers in his 10-year major-league career, including seven in 1987. Before the competition with Oakland was over, Hatcher would hit more home runs in the 1988 World Series than he had during the entire regular season. He would hit only two more home runs during the remainder of his career.

Although the Dodgers only led by two runs in the first inning, the game was shaping up to be a strange one. The American League home run champion Canseco had been hit on the arm. The Dodgers' leadoff hitter Sax was then hit on the shoulder the following inning, causing the umpire to warn the pitcher Stewart that any seemingly errant pitch that even remotely looked intentional would be cause for dismissal. Stewart then balked Sax to second base, and a man who had hit only one home run all season long, Hatcher, sent a Stewart fastball flying over the left-field fence, becoming only the 19th player in major-league history to hit a home run in his first World Series at-bat. As A's manager La Russa looked on without obvious emotion, right fielder Mike Marshall, the Dodgers' RBI leader during the regular season and himself a long-ball threat, stepped in to face the often-dominant Stewart. As he did so the crowd continued to cheer Hatcher's home run, prompting him to hop out onto the dirt beyond the dugout steps where he acknowledged the fans with a wave of his hands before disappearing into a sea of blue and white Dodger uniforms.

Whether it was due to the balk or perhaps the warning from umpire Harvey, or both, Stewart wasn't pitching like a two-time 20-game winner. However, in baseball redemption often comes quickly, and the pitcher had time to settle down before the game got away from him.

With Marshall, a six-foot-five, 215-pounder, coming to the plate, Stewart would have to pitch him carefully. In eight years as a member of the Dodgers, Marshall had slugged 126 home runs, an average of nearly 16 per season. Coming off a reasonably productive National League Championship Series against the Mets, driving in five runs with five singles, a double, and a triple, Marshall was eager to continue with his offensive heroics against the A's. Five pitches later, he struck out swinging on an off-speed split-finger fastball that dropped delicately like a hole in one as it flew over the plate.

Up next with two men out was the light-hitting center fielder John Shelby, a lifetime .239 hitter who batted 25 points higher than that in

1988. Shelby's hitting woes had reconvened during the playoffs, and he had batted just .167 with four hits in 27 at-bats against the Mets, knocking in three runs. Shelby did have 58 career home runs at the time he stepped in to face Stewart, including 22 in 1987, so the A's considered him a potential threat. Two pitches later he dribbled a slow roller to first baseman Mark McGwire, who sprinted to the bag a step ahead of Shelby to retire the side and eliminate any danger Shelby presented. Although the side was out, the damage to Oakland's psyche had been done. The Dodgers led 2-0 on the strength of Hatcher's improbable first-inning home run. As Shelby walked back toward the dugout to retrieve his glove, Hatcher sprinted out toward his position in left field, where the bleacher fans would offer a roar of approval to the man who had given them hope as Game One shifted to a higher gear.

CHAPTER 5

SLAM — 4-2

For Game One we were in the loge section on the first-base side. That was my first and only World Series game.

    I was a student at San Diego State University at the time, and my dad called me the day before the game and asked if I wanted to go. I said, "Yeah—of course!" I drove two hours home, we went to the game, and you know what happened.

    The Dodgers were completely overmatched. We all thought that, everybody thought that. We just went to the game because it was the World Series. I was a Dodger fan, of course, and I wanted them to win, but I didn't think they had a chance.

    What stood out to me were [Mark] McGwire and [Jose] Canseco—they were giants. Canseco hit that laser grand slam in the top of the second inning that hit the center-field camera. We looked at each other and said, "Oh, my gosh—it's gonna be a sweep." The sheer power of that home run was unbelievable. Hatcher's home run [in the first inning] was great, too, and it put everyone into a frenzy. But Canseco's home run was a bomb and I thought, "OK—that's it."

    Toward the end of the game I knew Eckersley was going to be coming in to pitch—he's always lights out. I was already thinking about going back to San Diego—I wasn't actually going to leave, because it was the World Series, but I thought the game was over. I stayed until the end, expecting to lose because I knew Eckersley was coming in. Gibson was not playing, of course, but I didn't know his status. When Gibson came out I knew he was a lefty going against a righty. I thought, "Maybe . . ." He was limping around on one leg or half a leg.

When he came out onto the on-deck circle, people started standing up and cheering. When he hit the home run, everyone went nuts. It was just insane. He could hardly walk, let alone run [around the bases].

The second he hit it, I knew it was out because the whole stadium erupted. The entire stadium was just shaking. Popcorn was flying. Food boxes were flying. Everything was flying around. I don't think I was even looking at the field because everyone was jumping up and down and hugging. It was crazy. It was awesome being there.

Afterward, we sat around for maybe half an hour and waited for people to leave. When we got to the parking lot, people were yelling and screaming and going crazy—it wouldn't end. The game was something I'll never forget. It was easily the best sports moment I've ever seen. —Brad Kuehfuss, 54, Glendora, California

---

With Steinbach's fly ball to the Dodger center fielder Shelby, who easily snagged it moving to his right for the third out to end a bases-loaded threat, Belcher was off the meat hook, at least temporarily. Not that he pitched the A's too terribly in his first-ever encounter with the club, just cautiously: After Henderson singled in the first inning with one away, a pitch got away from Belcher and struck Canseco on the forearm as he moved away from the plate. Then, McGwire walked. Parker did snatch a single, but no balls were hit too hard in the inning—even those that found their way into center fielder Shelby's glove were routine outs. Belcher had wanted little to do with either Canseco or McGwire, so the result of those at-bats was neither unexpected nor dispiriting. In fact, Belcher was probably glad to have those feared hitters out of the way, knowing they would likely come to bat only three more times if he pitched well enough the rest of the game. Still, his pitch count—29 after only half an inning—was ominous to Belcher as well as to Lasorda and the pitching coach, Ron Perranoski, who was closely monitoring his starter, and the pitcher needed a solid inning to halt the miasma. He had faced the toughest part of the A's lineup, a veritable wrecking crew, and coming up next were the bottom three men in the batting order: Glenn Hubbard, hitting .255 in his second-to-final season of play; Walt Weiss, batting .250 in his sophomore big-league season; and Dave Stewart, a 10-year veteran who did not bat during the regular season due to the American League's use of the designated hitter. Between the three of them they had logged a total of just six home runs all season long, a statistic that Belcher had no doubt been apprised of and one he took to heart.

Still, the duo of Canseco and McGwire was looming not far from the dugout steps, and Belcher, who considered himself fortunate to have escaped the first inning relatively unscathed, could not allow a repeat of that. He had to be sharp, it had to be then, and he couldn't afford to face either player with men in scoring position. One swift clout by either slugger and the Dodgers might never recover sufficiently enough to win the game and the World Series.

Between innings, it was backup catcher Rick Dempsey who warmed up Belcher as the right-hander prepared to face Oakland's big guns in the second inning, and that may not have been by accident. Dempsey, who went on to play 24 years in the major leagues and at that point was a veteran of two World Series [hitting .385 in 1983 against the Baltimore Orioles], was considered Belcher's on-field godfather, and he pointed to his left shoulder as Belcher threw a warmup pitch as if to remind the pitcher not to open up his delivery too soon.[1] Belcher would try to comply. When Dempsey was finished and Belcher was warmed, the regular catcher Scioscia walked onto the field and took his place behind home plate, ready for whatever might come.

"More than likely, I was just out there to warm him up until Scioscia got [his catcher's gear on] and went back out onto the field," Dempsey said. He added that occasionally during the season he did help Belcher with issues regarding his pitching delivery.

The 31-year-old Hubbard, up first in the second inning, had suffered a hamstring injury late in the season and had played in only four games down the month-long, regular season-ending stretch. Partially as a result, he was left off the playoff roster for the National League Championship Series against the Mets,[2] replaced in the lineup by Mike Gallego and Tony Phillips.

For Hubbard, the injury wasn't his first that season, nor was it the most serious one he experienced. During spring training he had suffered multiple fractures near his left eye when he was struck in the face by a pitched ball. During the World Series, just to be safe, Hubbard wore a special helmet that protected the entire left side of his face—including the eye, a batter's most important asset. When he watched Dodger Steve Sax narrowly escape the wrath of a Dave Stewart pitch that veered toward his head in the bottom half of the first inning, it had to be a stark reminder.

Despite sitting out the series with the Mets, Hubbard was considered a valuable commodity by virtue of his postseason experience as the 1988 World Series began. In 1982 Hubbard's Atlanta Braves had lost to the St. Louis Cardinals in the National League Championship Series, 3-0, and Hubbard went 2 for 9 with an RBI; his batting average during that forgettable series was a chintzy .222. Hubbard had not played since September 29 due to the hamstring injury, and because he had missed the A's recent 4-0 American League Championship Series drubbing of the Boston Red Sox, he figured to be somewhat rusty after a 16-day layoff since his final regular-season game.

Belcher greeted Hubbard with a fastball that drifted low for a ball. Two called strikes followed, the second hitting the outside corner of the strike zone, and Hubbard was in a hole, 1-2. On the next pitch, Hubbard hammered a line drive that the left fielder Hatcher caught on a bounce, hop-skipping as he did so and firing the ball back to the shortstop Griffin, who held Hubbard to a single. Just like that . . . one on base for the Oakland A's—and one of their weaker hitters making noise.

As he stood attentively on first base, hopeful that a teammate might drive him in to cut the Dodgers' lead in half, Hubbard had to be wondering one thing: how much longer would he continue to play a boy's game at a level that suited him. The answer, although he couldn't have known it for certain at the time, was . . . not long. Then in his 11th year as a major-league ballplayer, Hubbard would play one more season with the Oakland A's before retiring from baseball. There would only be 26 more hits, including 17 singles, six doubles, and three home runs, for the native of Hahn, Germany, whose middle name, curiously, sounded more American than German: Dee. His batting average that final season would be a disappointing .198, his worst campaign in the major leagues, almost 60 points lower than his 1988 batting average, and nearly 50 points below his career average. Perhaps that gloomy statistic and the absence of runs driven in—there were only 12 RBI in 1989—irretrievably soured him and hastened his departure from baseball. Whatever the reason, fourth-year player Gallego, who replaced Hubbard in the lineup after a hamstring injury sidelined him late in 1988, would start the 1990 season at second base following his teammate's retirement. Hubbard, meanwhile, would finish his respectable career by locking down the one important measure of success that up until then had eluded him in baseball: a World Series title in 1989.

Like the Dodgers' Hatcher, Walt Weiss, the second player up for Oakland that inning, was a contact hitter who thrived on high pitches, unlike many left-handed batters who preferred low pitches. The options for the A's with the switch-hitting Weiss at the plate were cut and dried: he could swing away for a base hit, he and Hubbard could play hit-and-run, and Weiss was also capable of bunting from both sides of the plate, either pushing the ball toward third base to move his teammate over or dragging it down the first-base line in quest of a hit. A trustworthy switch hitter, Weiss was batting from the left side of the plate with the right-hander Belcher throwing for the Dodgers.

Weiss's fledgling career had begun inauspiciously enough a year earlier when, on July 12, 1987, he entered a game the day before the all-star break as a pinch hitter and was promptly picked off base. A year later, he erased memories of that miscue by hitting a grand slam on the day before the all-star break; an unidentified woman who caught the home run ball presumptuously forwarded the orb to the Oakland dugout, mistakenly requesting that Mark McGwire autograph it.[3] It is not known which player, if either, complied: Weiss, who authored the home run, or McGwire.

Belcher started Weiss off with a fastball for a called first strike, followed by a pitch that moved outside for a ball. His third delivery caught the outside corner, and the umpire Harvey called it a strike—1-2. As the catcher Scioscia stole a long look toward the Dodger dugout with the expectation of receiving a sign from the pitching coach Perranoski, Weiss, who during one stretch that season had played 58 consecutive games at shortstop without committing an error in advance of receiving the American League's 1988 Rookie of the Year Award—the team's third consecutive honoree—stepped back into the batter's box. Belcher came at him again with a fastball that Scioscia snagged near the dirt, bringing the count to 2-2. Hubbard took a cautious lead as Weiss, a University of North Carolina alum, fouled off two more pitches before Belcher mowed him down with a forkball that arced over the plate before settling into Scioscia's glove for a called third strike.

With one out and the pitcher Stewart walking slowly toward the plate, the odds shifted in Belcher's favor. As they do now, American League pitchers deferred their at-bats to a designated hitter during the regular season. At that point, Stewart had only batted 51 times during his career—and not once since he left the Dodgers organization five years earlier. Additionally, he had not registered an official at-bat during the 1981 National League Division Series, the 1981 World Series, or the 1988 American League Championship Series. Belcher, who was aware of Stewart's inexperience as a hitter, knew that if he could retire Oakland's starter for the second out, he might escape the inning without facing either Canseco or McGwire, both of them prodigious hitters with men in scoring position.

Belcher's first pitch to his counterpart Stewart, who seven years earlier had tripled for one of only two extra-base hits recorded during his career, was a fastball at the letters that the pitcher chased and missed. Belcher returned to his stretch, then made a quick glance over to Hubbard at first base before taking his foot off the rubber and re-setting his pitching posture for the next delivery. Appearing relaxed as he enjoyed a lead with one out and the pitcher at bat, Belcher whizzed another fastball by Stewart in the exact same spot as the first one had been for another swinging strike that brought the count to 0-2. Then, to manager Lasorda's horror, Belcher took his foot off the gas.

Two balls out of the strike zone followed, then Stewart fouled a pitch off before Belcher, who seconds earlier had nearly picked Hubbard off first base, walked the pitcher on a 3-2 fastball that mirrored the two letter-high pitches that Stewart had swung at and missed earlier. Belcher, who by then had thrown 47 pitches, had squandered an opportunity for an easy inning by committing the cardinal sin: walking the opposing pitcher, this time with a man on base.

As Stewart gratefully trotted toward first base, with Hubbard moving over to second, two questions were left unanswered: why had Oakland manager La Russa not signaled for Stewart to bunt the runner into scoring position with only one out, although the walk would ultimately prove to be a more prodigious turn of events than a sacrifice? And, why had the eleemosynary Belcher nibbled around the corners of the strike zone rather than challenge the unpracticed Stewart with a series of fastballs down the middle, pitches he would probably not hit? Regardless of the answers to both of those questions, Belcher was in a jam with the top of the batting order poised to make a commotion.

With one out in the second inning, Oakland had already battled through the lineup, although the A's had little to show for the effort: three players left on base in the first inning, a pair of runners on base in the second, and the team still trailing 2-0. Up to bat walked Carney Lansford, who had opened the World Series by striking out looking against Belcher. The second time around, with Belcher no longer a mystery, Lansford was anxious to get on base with the big hitters coming up behind him.

For Belcher, Lansford was his last best hope to exit the inning undamaged—Henderson, Canseco, Parker, and McGwire would follow, a foursome that had hit a whopping 110 home runs during the 1988 season. Before retiring, those players would amass a remarkable 1,581 home runs between them—an average of 395 per slugger. Belcher clearly had a tough road ahead if he hoped to avoid a knockout punch from that intimidating triumvirate.

Before Lansford stepped in to bat, Perranoski walked from the Dodger dugout to the mound for a conference with the battery mates. A moment later, with Perranoski at least somewhat satisfied that Belcher should continue, he walked back to the dugout, more nervous than comforted by his summit. As he watched his coach exit toward the dugout, Belcher flipped the resin bag up and down a few times, nonchalantly lobbed it onto the dirt behind him, then took his position behind the pitching rubber, awaiting signals from his catcher. Scioscia's pitch strategy would have to be exceptional or the inning could explode.

Lansford, an excellent bunter and a first-pitch fastball hitter who had earned a reputation for hitting high pitches over the fence, took the first pitch from Belcher—a fastball outside—for a ball. He then fouled off a second pitch toward the A's dugout on the first-base side of the field, evening the count at 1-1. Finally, Belcher's wildness broke through as another fastball flew behind the surprised Lansford, who dropped his bat and ducked as Scioscia attempted to glove the ball before it bounced off his mitt into a slough of dirt behind the plate. Despite the two first-inning hit batters, one by each pitcher, and a subsequent warning to Stewart from home plate umpire Harvey, there was no thought of admonishing Belcher, as the likelihood that he threw at his opponent with two men on base was nil. Belcher was simply trying to fight his way out of a jam that threatened to break the ballgame open.

With the count 2-1, Belcher fired a slider away from Lansford and he was suddenly one pitch away from loading the bases. As he struggled to regain his composure, the crowd was becoming uneasy less than half an inning after Hatcher's blast had put them at ease; so was manager Lasorda, who at one point mumbled to himself in exasperation as his pitcher struggled on the mound. Then, with unusual suddenness for the early innings of a World Series first game, a telephone rang in the Dodger bullpen. Moving quickly to begin warming up was Tim Leary, an effective starter throughout the season whose numbers were impressive: 17 wins and a 2.91 ERA. As Leary rushed to loosen his arm, Lansford fouled off another pitch, making the count full. Seconds later, a high fastball

Jose Canseco demonstrates his powerful swing with the Oakland A's (National Baseball Hall of Fame).

sent him striding off to first base with a walk. Oakland had loaded the bases for the second time in two innings.

Since the World Series was first launched in 1903, only 18 players have hit grand slam home runs in the Fall Classic.[4] The first to do it was Elmer Smith of the Cleveland Indians, who achieved the feat on October 10, 1920, hitting his blast in the bottom of the first inning of Game Five off

Hall of Famer Burleigh Grimes of the Brooklyn Robins, forerunner to the Dodgers.[5] The most recent player to accomplish it was Alex Bregman of the Houston Astros on Oct. 26, 2019, in Game Seven. Others who drove in four runs during a World Series with a single swing include a host of recognizable names: Hall of Famers Tony Lazzeri, Mickey Mantle, and Yogi Berra, along with Gil McDougald and Bobby Richardson, all of them New York Yankees. Eight of the 20 players wore pinstripes.

Dave Henderson, the player up next in the A's Game One batting order, was no stranger to playoff series heroics. In the ninth inning of Game Five in the 1986 American League Championship Series, facing California Angels pitcher Donnie Moore with his team down 5-4, Henderson blasted a two-run shot that momentarily gave his Boston Red Sox the cushion, a lead they would relinquish in the bottom half of the inning. However, Henderson came back two innings later and put the Red Sox up for good with a sacrifice fly in the 11th inning that won the game. As a result of Henderson's inspiring performance, Boston won the championship series and Henderson went on to hit two more home runs in a losing 1986 World Series effort against the New York Mets.

With Leary continuing to warm up in the Dodger bullpen, Belcher started Henderson off with a slider that missed outside for a ball. Scioscia, hoping to head off a bases-loaded walk, scurried to the mound to confer with his pitcher, and after the short summit ended, Belcher fired a fastball that Henderson fouled off: 1-1. An off-speed curve missed outside for a ball, and at that point one thing was apparent: Belcher only had control of one pitch, his fastball, as he struggled to stay in the ballgame. The count was 2-1.

Dodger Stadium was by then covered in early-evening shadows, giving the hitters a distinct and advantage over pitchers, when Belcher came back at Henderson with a fastball that was low and out of the strike zone. The count was 3-1 and the rookie was in a big-league jam..

Sticking with the fastball, he delivered another one that caught the outside corner of the plate for strike two, followed by a fastball that Henderson mercifully missed for a third strike. Belcher, his manager Lasorda, who by then was sitting alone in the Dodger dugout and nervously pinching his lower lip, and the entire home crowd were momentarily relieved when the second out was recorded. Belcher was only one out away from getting out of the inning without a nick.

As he stood near the on-deck circle at Dodger Stadium, taking practice swings with the boisterous home crowd anxiously rooting against his powerful team, Jose Canseco was hoping to add his name to the exclusive list of World Series grand slam hitters. In his four seasons as a major leaguer, Canseco had never hit a grand slam, and with the bases loaded in Game One, with his team losing to the Dodgers, 2-0, Canseco was hopeful of turning the contest in Oakland's favor. What better way than to clear the bases with a single swing, something he would not do in a regular-season game until May 22, 1990—two years later. In his entire career Canseco would hit just six grand slams, a far smaller total of bases-loaded blasts than achieved by many players who hit fewer career home runs than Canseco and tying him for 236th place on the all-time major-league leaderboard,[6] well behind career leader Alex Rodriquez with 25.

Facing Canseco was a pitcher on the verge of a swift hook in his first-ever World Series game. At that moment in the second inning, Belcher had only recorded five outs. He had loaded the bases in both of the innings he had worked, and his pitch count was becoming more and more unsettling to both Lasorda and Perranoski. Perhaps most troubling, Belcher was facing one of the game's most prolific home run hitters, a man who had led the league in round-trippers that season. If he didn't bear down and extricate himself from the jam at once, there would be no third inning of work for Tim Belcher. Even if he did retire Canseco, the path to remaining in the game was a narrow one and fraught with thistles. Belcher was scheduled to bat fourth in the second inning. As ineffective as he was pitching, it was likely Lasorda would remove him for a pinch hitter sooner rather than later, especially if someone else got on base. Still, the mighty Canseco, the image of Fabio, Hulk Hogan, and Spanky McFarland all rolled into one, had to be contended with.

In all of baseball, few players have elicited as much emotion as Jose Canseco. A near-Hall of Fame player with a grand total of 462 home runs to his credit, he twice led the American League in home runs and once in RBI and was feared like the devil by opposing teams.

Jose Canseco Capas Jr. was born shortly before Independence Day on July 2, 1964, in Havana, Cuba, to Jose Canseco Sr., who had worked as an English professor in Cuba, and the former Barbara Capas. Born a twin, Canseco is two minutes younger than his brother Ozzie, who played baseball in the major leagues from 1990 to 1993—never hitting a single home run. His residency in Cuba was short-lived. After Fidel Castro rose to prominence in 1959, the Canseco family fled their home country six years later with no reasonable likelihood of finding living-wage work and little money in their pockets; young Jose was just nine months old at the time. Fortunately, Canseco's father found employment as a daytime filling station attendant and nighttime security guard, eventually rising to become an executive with Amoco Corp. in Florida, an oil and chemical company.

As a youngster, Jose attended Coral Park High School in Miami, Florida, where his sport of choice was baseball. He was so good, especially during the latter years of high school, that the Oakland A's drafted him in the 15th round, 392nd pick, of the 1982 Major-League Baseball June amateur draft. At the age of only 18, he played for two different affiliates within the Oakland organization: the Idaho Falls A's, a rookie-level team, batting .263 with two home runs, and the Miami Marlins, a Class A team, batting .111 with only one hit in nine at-bats—it wasn't a home run. Despite those modest numbers, the ever-upbeat Canseco was on his way to fame and fortune.

The following season Canseco played for two more teams, in Medford, Oregon, and Madison, Wisconsin, both at the Class A level, and he batted a cumulative .235 with 14 home runs and 50 RBI. Despite registering only 285 at-bats, Canseco's characteristic power was beginning to materialize.

He continued in Class A during the 1984 season, hitting 15 home runs with 73 RBI. The A's apparently liked what they saw and elevated him to the Class AA Huntsville Stars and the Class AAA Tacoma Tigers during the 1985 season. Combined, he hit 36 home runs, drove in 127 runs, and batted .333 with those teams, good enough for a brief call up with the major-league A's late in the 1985 season. While with the club for just 96 at-bats he nonetheless proved himself a worthy candidate for full-time employment with the big club, hitting five home runs—the equivalent of a 25-home run season—and batting .302.

It was smooth sailing for the up-and-coming slugger after that, and Canseco remained with the A's from 1986 through 1992, hitting 33 home runs and driving in 117 runs during his first full season with the club. For the next six years he was a mainstay with the organization, until Texas picked him up in 1992 and Boston three years after that. Stints with the Yankees and White Sox followed in 2000 and 2001 before a long slow slog through a series of independent minor-league venues began, including stops in San Diego, Sonoma, and Long Beach, California; Yuma, Arizona; Laredo and Ft. Worth, Texas; and Worcester, Massachusetts; and Pittsburgh, Pennsylvania. In all, he hit 462 major-league home runs, an additional 72 dingers in the minor leagues, and drove in a combined total of 1,677 RBI. His lifetime batting average through 17 major-league seasons was a respectable .266.

As he walked toward home plate on October 15, 1988, Canseco's life had been a cacophony of travel dates, airplane jaunts, unfamiliar cities, ballparks, and, ultimately, home runs. At that moment, Canseco, who after the season ended would be named the American League's Most Valuable Player, would do almost anything to record one of those signature blasts.

Whether it would appear at that moment depended largely upon Tim Belcher and his ability to control his secondary pitches, specifically the curveball and changeup. Thus far, that had not happened—his outing through one and two-thirds innings had been a cauldron of missed pitches, walks, and even a hit batter, although Belcher, who was not considered a strikeout pitcher, had recorded three K's early on in the game. He hoped to right the fast-sinking ship beginning with Canseco, who had a habit of sinking ships in his own right with big home runs. The muscular Cuban stepped into the batter's box with a visage of purpose, waved five practice swings in the direction of his counterpart Belcher, and stood at the ready for the most significant confrontation of the evening—at least thus far. Belcher wound up and delivered to the imposing Canseco.

The first pitch, a fastball, zoomed slightly high as Canseco crouched low to visualize the ball as it passed by him at eye level. The last thing the pitcher wanted was to fall behind in the count on a home run hitter with the bases loaded, forcing him to battle the feisty Canseco with the only pitch in his arsenal that appeared to be working—the fastball, a money pitch to home run hitters. However, that first pitch out of the strike zone may have been designed to feel out Canseco or perhaps tempt him to swing at a bad ball. Or, wasting the first pitch may have been planned to calm Belcher into effectiveness. Whatever the intent—perhaps the high fastball wasn't intentional at all—Canseco briefly stepped outside the batter's box, then back into it again. He stood semi-erect as the pitcher looked for signs from Scioscia, waved three more practice swings to remain loose, and waited for a pitch he hoped could be driven. It would come sooner than he expected.

From his perch atop the center-field fence, an NBC cameraman had a straightaway view, although distant, of the Oakland slugger standing alongside home plate. To him, the A's star must have looked normal-sized. What happened next was large, far from normal-sized. More than three decades later, Canseco's offensive attack is still discussed in the context of the overall excitement that Game One presented, mostly during three solitary innings: the first, the second, and the dramatic ninth.

With the count 1-0, Belcher delivered a fastball down the middle that Canseco blasted, sending it deep toward the crushed brick warning track that rimmed the outfield fence between the foul poles.

"And there's a drive to center, back goes Shelby to the wall, it is gone!" broadcaster Scully declared to his radio audience, many of whom were listening on their transistor receivers at Dodger Stadium. "Grand slam home run for Jose Canseco!"

Scully added, "Did he ever smoke it!"

As the ball shot like a frozen rope toward center field, with Canseco pausing momentarily to admire its flight, Shelby had sprinted back to the right of the 395-foot marker and toward the camera. The cameraman, perhaps anticipating a direct hit by the baseball, dipped the lens downward at the last second to protect the glass and the ball struck the top of the camera, bouncing down onto the ground and rolling between a pair of large flagpoles. As Canseco circled the bases to the delight of the relatively few Oakland fans who were in attendance, Shelby walked dejectedly back to his position in center field, his team trailing for the first time in the ballgame. For Canseco, the blast was, as former Dodger and two-time no-hit author Carl Erskine would call it, "one of those magic moments" in baseball. Erskine should know—on October 3, 1951, the longtime Indianan was warming up in the bullpen when Ralph Branca was asked to relieve Don Newcombe with Bobby Thomson coming to the plate. The rest is history

"It was hit hard," Hines, the Dodger hitting coach, said of Canseco's shot. "It was then that I realized it was going to be a battle to the end."

In one magnificent motion, Canseco had more than avenged Belcher for hitting him on the arm with a pitched ball in the first inning. In one fell swoop he had hit his first career grand slam, cleared the bases of his three teammates—Lansford, Stewart, and Hubbard—erased an early 2-0 A's deficit, and sent his team careening into the lead, leaving the hometown Dodgers wondering what had just happened.

Canseco had just happened, as he often did in 1988, and he commented on the home run in his unique style shortly after Game One was completed. "That's why power hitters are so well-paid," he said. "They can put the game away for you. People say power hitters are overpaid, overrated. That's bull. That's the man you want up there, that's the man who makes the big bucks."

Canseco, who wasn't through evaluating his grand slam, was unabashed in his self-praise.

"Did you see how *hard* I hit it?" he asked a reporter. "I hit it extremely hard." He added, "Hard enough."

"My dad was here today," Canseco continued. "Of all the power hitters we've got in Oakland, I'm the only one who's never hit a grand slam. My father's always telling me, 'When you gonna hit one? When you gonna hit one?' [I thought,] 'Sure, Dad, I'll hit one tonight.' When I hit it, the first thing that went through my mind was, 'Grand slam, national TV, my father's here to see it, I'm covered.'"[7]

As his shot rocketed toward the fence and the camera, Canseco had grinned, flipped the bat nonchalantly over his right shoulder, and clenched his fists above his shoulders in glee, much like another player would similarly celebrate later in the game. He then coasted around the bases, appearing to fight back a smile with each stride. When he crossed home plate and walked down the steps into the A's dugout toward an ocean of delighted faces, a smile finally broke broadly across his face. Seconds earlier, Canseco was greeted at home plate by Dave Stewart, Carney Lansford, and Glenn Hubbard, the three players he had just driven in to put his team ahead in one of the most important series of games they would ever play.

Six pitches later, with the count full, Belcher walked Dave Parker to keep the inning alive, with Parker trotting down to first base. In perhaps the evening's biggest anticlimactic moment, McGwire then approached the plate, bat in hand, with four runs in the bank and only Parker on base for him to potentially drive in. As Belcher watched the former USC all-American and American League Rookie of the Year make his way toward home plate, Lasorda sat quietly in the Dodger dugout, arms crossed and staring straight ahead, hoping perhaps that the dugout roof would somehow collapse in a heap, crushing him and ending his nationally televised spate of misery. As with most baseball-related miseries, it did not.

Instead, McGwire stepped in. At that point, Leary was still loosening up, joined in the bullpen by left-hander Ricky Horton, although Lasorda hoped his starter might finesse the slugger to get the final out, thus precluding his team from having to waste a pitcher with Belcher due to bat fourth in the second inning. Belcher got two quick strikes on McGwire, threw a high fastball that the slugger watched go by into Scioscia's mitt, then got him on a bouncer to shortstop Alfredo Griffin, who tossed the ball to the second baseman Sax for the force out. As they say in sports, however, the damage was done. With just one and one-half innings in the books the Oakland Athletics led the Los Angeles Dodgers, 4-1.

"It was probably one of the worst games I ever pitched on one of the biggest stages I ever pitched on," Belcher said of his short and inglorious start in Game One of the 1988 World Series, which was almost a losing effort. "But it also was the most enjoyable game I've ever been a part of because of the way it ended."[8]

Dempsey, the backup catcher, was less critical of his teammate. "He made one bad pitch and it hit the camera in center field with the bases loaded," he said. "He had a pretty good game with the exception of that one inning."

One critically important inning. Less than two frames into the ballgame, Belcher would not throw another pitch.

CHAPTER 6

THE PRELUDE

In August 1988, the Dodgers held a lottery—I mailed a postcard to the team, and all of a sudden two tickets arrived in the mail. The tickets were $60 each. I took the day off, we dropped our two kids off at the in-laws' house, and my wife and I went to Game One. We stopped and got a few souvenirs before going inside rather than pay ballpark prices. I bought a World Series pennant.

I was excited to be there because it was the World Series, and I was happy that the Dodgers had beaten the Mets [in the National League Championship Series]. I didn't think they were going to do that well against Oakland.

They were leading 2-0, then Canseco hit the grand slam. It was coming right at us and it barely cleared the fence. It was a shot. Then, the Dodgers got another run and it was a one-run ballgame.

Leaving early was never a thought for us—that was not even a possibility. It was a one-run game, for crying out loud—anything can happen.

We probably had the best seats in the house to watch Gibson's ball go over the right-field fence, and when he connected my initial thought was, "OK—we're tied." It took me an extra second to realize, "It's over—we're done here!" We watched him run around the bases.

We stuck around for about an hour—nobody wanted to leave. Finally, we walked down to the Dodger dugout just to see what was going on. Everyone was just milling around. People were so happy. It was pandemonium. You knew you were part of something pretty darn special.

[Of all the sporting events I've ever been to, Game One] was Number 1. —Ross Peabody, 65, Carlsbad, California

---

With the 1988 World Series then only a glimmer, Dodger catcher Mike Scioscia dug in at home plate against fire balling Dwight Gooden of the Mets, one of the premier pitchers in all of baseball. It was Game Four of the 1988 National League Championship Series, a week before the World Series would begin, and the Mets had won two of the first three contests by scores of 3-2 and 8-4. A victory at home in Game Four would all but secure the New Yorkers' bid to play in the World Series against another California team, the Oakland A's.

Through eight innings the mild-mannered, sometimes-mild-hitting Scioscia had been hitless, striking out in the first inning, lining out in the fourth, and grounding into a double play in the sixth. His team was also struggling offensively, trailing 4-2 when the Darby, Pennsylvania, native came to bat with center fielder John Shelby standing on first base following a walk. The workmanlike Scioscia was ready for whatever Gooden might dish up, and he drilled the 6-foot-2 right hander's first delivery for a shot deep to right field that Strawberry watched soar over the fence for a home run. In the unlikeliest fashion, the Dodgers had tied the game with their necks in a noose and would win the contest in 12 innings, 5-4. Instead of the Mets leading the series 3-1 with Game Five scheduled to be held on their home field, the match was tied 2-2.

"[It] very well may have been [the turning point of the post season]," Dodger general manager Clair said of Scioscia's home run. "[And] John Shelby's walk right before that. If Shelby doesn't walk before Scioscia's homer, it's a different story."

The Dodgers would win two of the next three games and the series, moving on to the World Series.

"I got a pitch from Doc [Gooden] that was middle-in and ended up hitting it out of the park," Scioscia said. "It was pure luck. What's eerie about it is that it was at Shea Stadium, 50,000 people, but it got so quiet that I could hear my spikes on the dirt like I was the only one out there. It was surreal [how] the place got that quiet."[1]

Lasorda added: "Scioscia's home run was, I think, more important to our club than Gibson's home run in the World Series. [If] Scioscia doesn't hit that home run, we may not have even been in the World Series. Every time he hit a home run it was a big one."[2]

Including the NLCS, Scioscia would hit four home runs during 1988 and just 33 through the remainder of his 13-season career. His blast against the Mets would be the most consequential one in a year that would see him hit .257, well below expectations [he had hit .296 in 1985]. Needless to say, Scioscia could be a big-game player.

"Mike was so solid in every way—knowing the game, knowing the pitchers, and loving the game," Claire said. "He was born to catch."

Certainly, Orel Hershiser's complete-game shutout victory in Game Seven of the NLCS was a significant moment for the team, but before that was Scioscia's big moment. His home run stopped the Mets' momentum, turned the series around, and motivated his teammates to win two of the next three games and eventually the series. Scioscia would bat .364 in the process, experiencing success at the plate that he would not see in the World Series. Against Oakland he hit just .214 with three singles and one RBI. Nonetheless, he had done his part in turning around the NLCS so that his Dodger teammates could taste the joy of a 1988 World Series experience.

Fast forward to Game One, where Belcher was struggling on the mound.

"Belch threw the ball well," former Oakland reliever Honeycutt said. "We had the lead [against him], but we didn't do a whole lot. He kept [the Dodgers] in the game."

As his team was when Scioscia turned things around in the NLCS, the Dodgers were again trailing 4-2, this time on the strength of Jose Canseco's grand slam home run in the second inning. They needed a catalyst, but the team's usual catalyst, Kirk Gibson, was nowhere to be seen. Unless that changed, someone else would have to step forward and get the job done. But who?

Would that it were Steve Yeager, the Dodgers' personable catcher from 1972 to 1985 and Scioscia's predecessor. Just two years into retirement, Yeager was regretting his decision to leave the game, and he made it known publicly before Game One.

"I think I can still play, and I'd like a chance to find out if I can," said the 39-year-old, a World Series co-MVP in 1981 with two home runs. "I don't like the way I left the game. It wasn't my decision, and I want it to be my decision. I want to have the satisfaction of knowing I gave it one last shot."[3]

The World Series does that to ballplayers. It makes them regret having left the game, especially when their former team is basking in the limelight with a World Series ring on the line.

Traded from the Dodgers to the Seattle Mariners after the 1985 season, Yeager was benched by the team's manager, Dick Williams. On the season he hit only .208, playing in fewer than one-third of the team's 162 games. He hit two home runs—his high in the major leagues was 16 in 1977—and drove in a modest 12 runs compared with a high of 55 in 1977. At the age of 37, Yeager was through.

"I'm telling you, I'm ready to go out there and play again," he said. "I really think I am."[4]

Unfortunately for Yeager, his position behind the plate was then in the capable hands of the man he mentored: Scioscia. With Scioscia catching, there would be no comeback for Yeager.

As Tim Belcher crossed the white chalk line that ran up the third-base line toward the outfield pavilion and made his way toward the Dodger dugout, the world he had put behind him, at least for the next two hours, was changing. Ronald Reagan, who some believe was among the greatest U.S. presidents ever to occupy the Oval Office, was preparing to leave government forever; his successor, Vice-President George H.W. Bush, was vigorously campaigning for the nation's highest office, a position he would win in a landslide election just three weeks later. A month after that, a Pan American World Airways 747 would be downed by terrorists in Lockerbie, Scotland, killing 270 people. That same month, smooth-throated Roy Orbison would die of a heart attack at the age of 52, just two days after his final performance. His first wife had died in a motorcycle accident, and two sons perished in a house fire.

At that moment, the only thing Belcher was concerned about was the Oakland A's. As he entered the Dodger dugout he did not yet know that his concern for the remainder of the evening would be focused from that same dugout rather than from the pitching mound, where a teammate would assume the reigns in the third inning. That pitcher was Tim Leary, a 29-year-old right-hander who had joined the club the previous season. Leary recorded one save that first season with the Dodgers and none during the rest of his career. Still, Lasorda was calling upon Leary to stop the onslaught and put the Dodgers on firmer footing. Over the three innings he would work, Leary would do just that, facing 14 batters, allowing two hits, striking out two batters, and allowing zero runs.

Noticeably absent in recent days had been another Dodger relief pitcher, Jay Howell, who left the mound during an NLCS game against the Mets after umpires confiscated his glove, which they contended held pine tar. Howell explained that he had used the substance to enhance his grip on the baseball during the cool, blustery weather of Game Three, which the Mets won 8-4. The following day, Baseball Commissioner Bart Giamatti suspended the pitcher for three days, leaving the Dodgers shorthanded in the bullpen. At the same time, Howell conceded he had intentionally violated the rule prohibiting a pitcher from using any foreign substance while pitching. In admitting to the offense, he equivocated to his critics, most of them residing in and rooting for Oakland, by calling the rule a bad one. He added that he hoped the controversy was over.

Dodger fans hoped so as well, and they hoped Howell's suspension would have no prolonged ill effects on the team's World Series effort. After all, during the 1988 season Howell, the team's most effective relief pitcher, earned 21 saves, few by today's standards but more than any other relief pitcher had logged for the team in a decade. His record was solid 5-3 with a minuscule 2.08 earned run average, and he had recorded 70 strikeouts in 65 innings pitched as well. The team would need his services if they hoped to defeat the powerful A's.

"We didn't have a strategy [for beating the A's]," Lasorda said. "We did a lot of praying. Our team was nowhere near as talented as some of the other teams I managed. They were a bunch of guys who loved each other, worked hard with each other, and they did everything they could to satisfy the manager and the coaches."

As the Series approached, things only got worse for Howell. After losing the first game against the Mets and awakening the next morning to read that third-year Mets pitcher David Cone had penned a column calling Howell "a high school pitcher,"[5] then suffering through the pine tar incident and eventual suspension, Oakland designated hitter Don Baylor attacked Howell.

"What's he ever done?" Baylor wondered. "He couldn't save games over here [Howell left the A's in 1987 after spending three seasons there, joining the Dodgers just in time to make it to the World Series], so they got rid of him.

"We want him in the game, all right,"[6] Baylor added with a touch of sarcasm—for the Dodgers.

Howell, who had suffered through a rough week, responded cautiously. "Just because Don Baylor says something about me doesn't mean I have to say something about Don Baylor," he said. "I think he's a class guy. Don can say anything he wants about anybody. I just don't think it necessitates a comment from me."[7]

Baylor's apparent anger may have been festering for a while. After he earlier went on record as saying he preferred to face the Mets in the World Series rather than the Dodgers, reporters quoted Howell as exclaiming, "Do we have to apologize to Don Baylor for being here?" While Howell denied saying that, Baylor was upset nonetheless. He may have escalated things and made his comments because of what he believed Howell had said—or did he?

During Game One of the World Series announcer Joe Garagiola speculated that perhaps Baylor was trying to take the pressure off

Oakland's premier sluggers Canseco and McGwire, keeping them out of the limelight and enabling them to concentrate on playing baseball rather than interacting with the news media. Whatever the reason, the media began following Baylor around after he commented about Howell, while Canseco and McGwire were largely left to focus on baseball rather than interviews. Perhaps the alleged ploy did what it was intended to do.

Still, Baylor got the Dodgers' goat, causing several of them to offer their take on the situation. One was Dodgers infielder/outfielder Mickey Hatcher. "They can say whatever they want," said Hatcher. "If they want to light our fire, let 'em go ahead. We feed off publicity like that."[8]

In the end, Howell tried to diffuse the situation before the first game began, saying that as far as he was concerned, the two were still friends. He wondered if Baylor was perhaps yanking his chain.

"Clearly, there was an intensity that one would expect in any World Series, but not any different, in my memory, than some of the things that were involved in '77, '78, or '81 when we reached the World Series," Claire said. "Everything rises to a different pitch. Three of the people who were contributing for us—Alfredo [Griffin], the shortstop, Jay [Howell], the closer, and Mike Davis [were former A's]. And you had the Oakland team—Don Baylor was a friend. But those friendships are set aside now that it's time to play the game."

Stewart's second inning of work was a relatively uninterrupted one, at least compared with his first inning, as he allowed only a two-out, full-count line-drive single to right field by the weak-hitting Dodgers shortstop Alfredo Griffin before retiring pinch hitter Danny Heep, who batted for Belcher, on a groundout to the shortstop Walt Weiss, who looked at second in anticipation of forcing out Griffin before firing the ball across to McGwire at first base to get out of the inning easily enough. That Heep failed to beat out a hit was no surprise—Lasorda once said that if Heep ever challenged a pregnant woman to a foot race, he would finish third.

With two long innings in the books, a new Dodger pitcher prepared to face his first A's batter in the top of the third inning, hoping to stem the onslaught of Oakland baserunners that had so far swept across the

Dodger Stadium base paths. To the team's dismay, the third inning, like the first two, would begin in disquieting fashion for the Dodgers, whose early momentum had disappeared with the speed of Jose Canseco's second-inning rocket drive toward John Steinbeck's stately and picturesque San Gabriel Mountains.

CHAPTER 7

THE CALM

I had grown up going to Dodger games with my father and brothers; we had never been to a World Series game before. My father got four tickets, so he, my sister, my twin brother, and I attended. I think we sat in the upper deck above the broadcast booth on the third-base side of the stadium, about equal with third base. I remember my father telling us the tickets were expensive.

The A's had the best reliever in the game—Dennis Eckersley—and had a great team that year. They had more than 100 wins and were predicted to win [the World Series]. At the same time, the Dodgers had Orel Hershiser, who had set the all-time record for consecutive scoreless innings and was the dominant pitcher in the majors. I was hopeful.

Kirk Gibson was one of the Dodgers' top offensive weapons and was unable to play due to injury. The A's took an early lead, and when Eckersley came in to close the game in the bottom of the ninth, I thought the game was over. My father had a habit of leaving Dodger games early when he thought the outcome was certain so that we could beat the crowd and get home at a decent time. He suggested we should leave because he believed the game was over and the Dodgers were certainly going to lose. My brother and I convinced him to stay since it was the first World Series game we had ever been to. We were so happy we stayed.

Gibson could barely walk. He hobbled like an old man who needed either a cane or a wheelchair, but he was the heart of the team. He had led the Dodgers all year, particularly late in the season, and the crowd went crazy when he was announced. Everyone was on their feet and the stadium was electric. He looked terrible early in the at-bat, swinging and missing badly and looking very sore due to his injuries. He couldn't run, and he looked like his swing was affected as well. He was down 0-2 and worked the count to 3-2. Everyone was on the edge of their seats.

I remember the crack of the bat—it was a very well-hit ball and quickly made it into the right-field bleachers. I hugged my dad and then my brother, then my sister. I have this memory as Gibson rounded first and was hobbling toward second that he pumped his arm several times—I think he was as shocked as all of us that with his injuries he could muster a home run against the best closer in the game.

It was unbelievable. I have never been in a venue so loud, so crazy. Everyone was jumping and screaming and hugging. We had just seen a miracle. It was amazing. Everyone kept screaming and yelling and cheering for a long time. No one was headed to their cars—we were all caught up in the magic of the moment.

I have never experienced anything before or since that was anywhere close to this moment. Being there was fantastic—I was at Dodger Stadium for Clayton Kershaw's no-hitter in 2014, and there was no comparison. Nothing compares to this moment—it truly was an unbelievable, magical, once-in-a-lifetime event. —Keith Merkley, 59, Doha, Qatar

---

Tim Leary's entry into Game One was monumental, at least for him. At age 29 and with seven years of major-league experience behind him, the journeyman pitcher had never appeared in a World Series game. After Game One, there would be one more pitching opportunity for Leary in the Series, and he would finish the two games with a cumulative World Series ERA of 1.35; in contrast, his earned run average in two appearances against the Mets during the NLCS—the career starter was 0-1 working strictly in relief and looked like a fish out of water—was 6.23. The series against Oakland was Leary's opportunity to shine on a major stage before leaving the Dodgers for good the following season and bouncing around the major leagues with four more clubs, then retiring in 1994 with a 78-105 career record and a 4.36 ERA.

Facing Belcher during the early innings, Oakland had loaded the bases twice, sending 14 men to the plate—four of whom eventually scored. It was Leary's charge to close the flood gates and restore some order to the game and the World Series, at least from the Dodgers' perspective.

As the Goodyear blimp floated listlessly overhead, Leary slowly made his way to the pitching mound. By then the sky was ink black, the tricky late afternoon shadows that so often baffled hitters were gone, and the bright bank of stadium lights was fully operational as Terry Steinbach stepped in to face the opposing pitcher. Leary's first pitch to Steinbach was a high fastball that missed the strike zone. Five pitches later, Steinbach drilled another fastball that Hamilton tried to backhand but instead deflected at third base, the ball eventually being picked up by the shortstop Griffin. Just like that the A's, with nobody out and their ninth runner on base in just two-plus innings, were knocking on the Dodger door.

"We weren't the best [team]," Dodgers utilityman Tracy Woodson said. "We had really good pitching and we played really good defense. If you looked up and down the lineup, you weren't terrified. But I'll tell you what: the guys on the bench were really good teammates, and they were ready whenever their name or number was called. We liked each other. We got along—I really believe that the chemistry of that team was the best I'd ever been on."

Glenn Hubbard, who with Steinbach on base was not considered a hit-and-run threat, stepped into the box next and promptly lined a shot between Hamilton and Griffin that bounced to the left fielder Hatcher, a single that sent Steinbach coasting over to second. With 10 batters reaching base and only two-plus innings completed, the A's appeared to be in business. Leary, like his predecessor Belcher had been for most of his short duration on the mound, was in serious trouble.

Fortunately for Leary, the bottom of the A's lineup was due up, led by shortstop Walt Weiss. Hoping his infielder might produce some offense, Weiss's manager La Russa stood in the Oakland dugout, hands on his hips, calm and collected as usual.

Orel Hershiser at Bowling Green University (courtesy of Bowling Green University).

Weiss had hit .333 during the American League Championship Series and at that moment was not considered a threat to bunt the ball. After fouling a pitch to the first baseman Stubbs, Weiss lifted a fly ball to shallow left field where Hatcher and Shelby converged, with Hatcher making the easy catch. He then flipped the ball back to the infield while the runners held at first and second.

Leary breathed a sigh of relief as the pitcher Stewart, who had not batted all season long before the World Series, walked slowly to the plate. In fact, Stewart had not batted since 1985, and Leary, aware of his counterpart's unfamiliarity with the hickory, greeted him with a pitch that sank low across the plate for a ball. Oddly, on that first pitch Stewart showed no sign of bunting his teammates over to second and third.

Stewart swung at the next pitch and missed it, evening the count at 1-1. With La Russa gyrating signals, Stewart then squared to bunt and fouled a ball that Stubbs retrieved near the first-base line: 1-2. Leary followed with a perfect fastball on the outside corner that Stewart watched whiz by for a called third strike, and things suddenly looked considerably brighter for Leary, who moments earlier was more than likely reminiscing about his poor showing against the Mets during the NLCS and hoping he wouldn't repeat it.

Hoping he *would* repeat was the leadoff hitter Lansford, who had struck out in the first inning and walked in the second, both times against Belcher. As Lasorda paced in the Dodger dugout, Leary greeted Lansford, who had 90 hits during the first two months of the season and just 65 over the last four, with a split-finger fastball that missed the outside corner for a ball. After Lansford fouled a ball into the crowd along the first-base side, Leary came back with a fastball that the former batting champ chopped on several bounces to the shortstop Griffin, who took two steps to his left and danced upon the second-base bag for the third out. The Dodger Stadium faithful, which moments earlier were perched on the edges of their seats, could suddenly relax. Leary, a successful starter for the entire season, had stepped out of his comfort zone to relieve the struggling Belcher and retire the A's, although not without some nervous moments. Through three innings the A's, who had quickly deposed the starting pitcher Belcher, had stranded five runners on the base paths—three of them in scoring position. Still, the Dodgers, who had jumped to the early lead on Hatcher's unlikely first-inning home run only to see Canseco erase it with one mighty swing of the bat, were within striking distance. What's more, Leary, as a starter, could comfortably work an undetermined number of innings if required, depending, of course, upon Lasorda's need to pinch-hit for him should the Dodgers threaten to score some badly needed runs. As the Dodgers trotted off the field to bat for the third time in Game One, the ball, so to speak, was in their court.

Runs were not forthcoming in the third inning. The Dodgers did manage to put Mickey Hatcher on first base with a walk, however fly balls to deep right and left field by Sax and Stubbs—Stubbs's ball traveling to the fence—and a lineout to third by the right fielder Marshall ended any hope the team had of getting something going. Instead, with a third of the game completed, the A's remained in the driver's seat with Leary returning for his second inning of work.

Throughout the season the A's power had been clearly evident, and throughout the first three innings it was underscored. Things wouldn't change much in the fourth. Leading off against Leary was Dave Henderson, a first-pitch hitter appearing in his second World Series—he had batted .400 with two home runs playing for Boston in the 1986 Fall Classic. With Kirk Gibson standing in the far corner of the Dodger dugout wearing a warm-up jacket and still not expected to play, Leary blew a fastball that Henderson sliced down the right-field line, bouncing over the short blue fence and into the stands for a ground-rule double—his second hit of the evening. The A's suddenly had their 11th man on base as Lasorda, traversing the Dodger dugout while muttering to pitching coach Ron Perranoski, pondered a thus far-elusive strategy to silence the powerful Oakland A's bats.

As Henderson adjusted his stirrups and took a short lead off second base, Leary stood on the rubber and prepared to face Jose Canseco, who was standing at home plate with four RBI to his credit. Five pitches and an attempted pickoff later, Canseco bounced a ball to Griffin at short, who threw to Sax at second as Henderson broke for third. Sax chased him down and tagged him on the seat of his pants for the first out. With careless base running the A's had run themselves out of a potential big inning.

With Oakland's sails deflated, Dave Parker dribbled a comeback nubber that Leary threw into right field. As Marshall ran down the ball,

Canseco coasted into third and Parker, who had ambled his 230-pound frame into second, was called out for running inside the base path and interfering with Stubbs at first; in a double whammy, Canseco was ordered back to first base. The dual gaffes—sloppy base running by Henderson and Parker—loomed large.

After Canseco stole second base, another gaffe that effectively took the bat out of Mark McGwire's hands, Leary walked the slugger intentionally. Terry Steinbach then struck out swinging, stranding McGwire at first and Canseco at second and completing the A's fourth-inning collapse. As the Dodgers dodged another bullet, it was clear that their pitching had begun to come around. Still, the team needed to score some runs. With the Athletics' ace Stewart reasonably in command, the question Lasorda needed to answer was: how?

CHAPTER 8

BEFORE THE STORM

We were sitting in the left-field pavilion. I had been following the team and was really excited to be going to a World Series game. It was the first and only World Series game I've been to.

The one thing that drove me crazy was all of the people who were leaving early. My thinking was, "You're at a World Series game—you don't leave until it's over." We could see the taillights in the parking lot and the stadium was emptying out—there were lots of empty seats [late in the game]. I couldn't believe it. I would never leave ANY baseball game early.

I just hoped the Dodgers would come back and win the game. When Gibson hit the home run it was just amazing. You could hear the stadium roar, and I thought, "All you stupid people out in the parking lot . . ." During one of the best moments in baseball history, people were leaving the stadium. They all missed it. Just to see Gibson limp out there, barely able to walk, then to hit the home run was unbelievable.

We stayed at the ballpark for about 40 minutes afterward and people were going crazy—it was awesome. It was the greatest [sports] moment [I've ever seen]. I don't think anything could top it. —Susan Colias, 66, Chino Hills, California

As the playoffs shifted from New York to Oakland following the Dodgers' dramatic seven-game NLCS victory over the Mets, expectations of

Mark McGwire as a member of the 1984 U.S. Olympic team (courtesy of the University of Southern California).

the team capturing a second consecutive post-season series were lowered—by the Dodgers themselves. Assenting to popular opinion, the team embraced the increasingly accepted notion that Oakland held all the cards heading into their highly anticipated best-of-seven-games head-to-head confrontation. The same had been said before the series against the Mets began, and at least for seven games the underdog status seemed to suit the Dodgers. In light of that it made perfect sense for the team to again accept that inferior role, hoping to motivate the players to perform above their acknowledged capabilities.

"If I had my choice of being the overwhelming favorite or the slight underdog, I'll take the underdog any day," the projected Game One starting pitcher Belcher said. "We seem to do well in that role."[1]

So far. But would it benefit them twice in succession, this time against an even more powerful and aggressive Oakland Athletics team? The Dodgers believed the psychology might work.

"I don't think anyone is going to fall over in their seat if Oakland beats us," Belcher continued. "But if we beat them, whether it takes seven games or seven years, people will be very, very surprised. So where's the pressure there?"[2]

Rejecting both the notion and the intended trickery was A's manager La Russa, who at least in public did not accept the allegation that Kirk Gibson's absence from the starting lineup or any other perceived Dodger shortcoming necessarily spelled doom for the team as it headed into the World Series.

The war was on, with the battle on the field scheduled to begin in earnest later that afternoon. Hatcher, ever the firecracker, fired back, suggesting the Oakland players simply keep their mouths shut in the event the Series didn't turn out how they hoped.

Going into the World Series, the Dodgers' argument appeared to hold the most water. They had won their division by seven games, struggling at every turn to maintain the advantage over others in their division as the season wound down. Oakland, meanwhile, had won their division by almost twice that number—13 games, coasting toward the finish line at season's end. It took all the Dodgers had to defeat the Mets in seven games, while Oakland won the ALCS in four games and spent the next two days resting up while at least mentally preparing for whomever they might face in the next and final round. The Dodgers hit a paltry .214 in the Mets series while Oakland batted a shade below .300 against the Red Sox. Certainly, Oakland was the odds-on favorite to emerge victorious, although odds often take a back seat where heart is involved. If anyone on either team had heart it was Belcher, a former Oakland property who came into his own after joining the Dodgers in 1987.

"I've never attempted to carry out a vendetta on the A's for giving up on me," he said. "They did what they thought they had to do. They never gave me a shot in the big leagues, but I never gave them a reason to believe I'd change."[3]

Whether he truly *had* changed was not in dispute. However, just how much would be litigated in earnest on the playing field later that day. Until then, the war of words continued, bouncing from player to player and up the line to the manager with the ultimate test to be carried out on ball fields in Oakland and Los Angeles.

Through the first 3-1/2 innings the Dodgers had been held in check, and the trend would continue for several more innings. In the bottom of the fourth, Stewart retired the Dodgers in order, striking out two batters. Leary returned for his final inning of work and retired the A's in order in the fifth, striking out one and getting two outs on ground balls. The Dodgers managed a walk in their half of the fifth but once again could not generate a run. In that inning, Tracy Woodson pinch-hit for the pitcher Leary, grounding into a fielder's choice. Leary left the game with three innings to his credit and no runs allowed, effectively keeping his team in contention after Belcher's unanticipated early departure.

For Woodson, who was 26 at the time, the at-bat marked his first-ever taste of World Series action. There would be three more at-bats for Woodson in the Series, none resulting in base hits, although he did collect an RBI. He admitted he was slightly nervous during his first time to the plate in Game One.

"It was an exciting time," said Woodson. "I was nervous the first time I stepped in, then I kind of settled down.

"I grounded into a force play, went to second base on a wild pitch, got stranded there, and that was it. It was a little chilly that night and I was the only one wearing a jacket at home plate after the home run by Gibson." Woodson, who hit his first major-league home run off Nolan Ryan, greeted Gibson at home plate with a bear hug from behind.

Brian Holton, a six-foot-two, 190-pound right-hander in his fourth and final year with the Dodgers, worked the sixth inning in relief of Leary and retired three of Oakland's most effective hitters in succession: Lansford, Henderson, and Canseco. Holton would pitch one more inning that day, then not see action the rest of the Series; he would never pitch for the Dodgers again, joining the Baltimore Orioles in 1989 and retiring from the game in 1990 after just 58 innings pitched over six major-league seasons.

"Holton had some huge, huge games for us," Woodson said.

Thanks to Leary's effectiveness in relief, the Dodgers had kept the game close. Oakland had been limited—so to speak—to Canseco's grand slam home run, while Stewart had not allowed a run since Hatcher's two-run homer in the first. With three innings left to play, the Dodgers were down to their final nine outs. It was managerial master against managerial master, brute strength against cunning and heart. Just who would win Game One of the 1988 World Series was anybody's guess.

CHAPTER 9

CLOSING IN — 4-3

I remember very clearly that [the Dodgers] were losing, and a couple of batters before Kirk Gibson came up my dad wanted to leave. He wanted to beat the traffic—he had to get up early the next morning for work and was concerned about spending an hour and a half in the parking lot. My dad had a lot more adult issues to be concerned about than I had, but I remember looking at him and thinking, "The game's not over yet!" As a six-year-old, leaving was a non-starter. I remember standing my ground as much as a six-year-old could, turning away, and silently hoping he wouldn't pick me up and make us leave the ballpark. I wore him down and he was resigned to staying.

We were sitting in the left-field loge level just beyond third base. I'm not sure I was aware that Kirk Gibson wasn't going to play, but I remember being struck by all the cheering when he came up to bat. I looked at my dad and he said, "Oh, [Gibson] isn't supposed to play." Then, he hobbled out there, the home run happened, and the place exploded. My dad and I were cheering.

We stayed around for a few minutes afterward, and then practicality set in as my dad had to be up in a few hours. We walked to the parking lot and got stuck in bumper-to-bumper traffic in the stadium. The car overheated and steam started coming out from under the hood. My dad pulled into a [gas] station in the parking lot and had the radiator filled. But something was broken and everything leaked out. So, we sat there for 20 minutes listening to everyone cheer as they drove past us out of the parking lot.

We called a tow truck but the tow truck couldn't get to us until everyone was out of the stadium. They put the car up on the tow truck, took it back to our home, and we got back at around 1 A.M. We were among the last fans to leave the stadium. It's kind of funny that my dad wanted to leave early to beat traffic, and because the car overheated we were among the last people to exit the ballpark.

That game was the number one sporting event I've ever attended.
—*Evan Wagner, 39, Culver City, California*

As Dodger catalyst Mickey Hatcher moved energetically toward home plate to begin the sixth inning, a lull was in force. His team had managed just one hit, Alfredo Griffin's single in the second inning, since Hatcher had connected for a two-run homer in the first inning. In all, his team had managed just two hits in the ballgame. Clearly, their nemesis Stewart had regained his footing since starting off rocky, although the former Dodger had struck out only three batters through the first five innings.

Offensively, Oakland hadn't fared much better. Since Jose Canseco's second-inning grand slam his teammates had collected just two singles and a double and had managed just six hits in the contest. Like Stewart had done after his rough early innings, Dodger reliever Leary had slowed the A's momentum while keeping his team in the game, pitching three workmanlike innings without allowing a run.

"From an offensive standpoint, a huge part of what happened to us was that we had swept the Red Sox in the ALCS and the Dodgers were coming off an emotional series to beat the Mets," Carney Lansford said. "After we swept the Red Sox, all we did was take batting practice—we never played any intrasquad games. I think that affected us the entire series. Also, I was surprised at how well [the Dodgers'] starting pitchers threw the ball. Obviously, Orel Hershiser was a great pitcher. I don't even remember the names of the others, but they threw better than I thought they'd throw."

To the feisty Hatcher leading off the inning, none of that mattered. In Hatcher's mind the rest of the game began with him, and whether the

Dodgers won or lost the World Series depended solely upon how they performed from then on out—not on any success they had achieved earlier, which was minimal.

With the count to him 1-0, Hatcher lashed Stewart's second pitch on a fly to Dave Henderson in center field, and Henderson easily flagged down the ball. One away.

Next up was the right fielder Mike Marshall and Stewart started him off with a curveball that flew down the middle for a strike. Marshall tapped both shoes with his bat, stepped out of the batter's box to collect himself, then stepped back in to await the next pitch. The ritual didn't seem to matter as he fouled off Stewart's next delivery, leaving himself in a hole at 0-2 with time for the Dodgers slowly running out.

After a fastball faded outside, Marshall lined Stewart's next pitch for a single to right field that Canseco caught on a bounce and lobbed back to the infield. With one away, the Dodgers were finally making some noise.

With Marshall standing on first base the Dodger Stadium crowd, which had become uneasy as the innings ticked away, was becoming boisterous, roaring its approval. Marshall stared dispassionately toward home, removing his batting glove as the left-handed John Shelby stepped in to face Stewart.

After swinging at a strike, Shelby drilled Stewart's next pitch, a fastball, off the pitching mound into center field, where Henderson picked it up and threw it back toward the infield to hold Marshall at second following the team's second hit of the inning. In two swings of the bat, the Dodgers had doubled their hit production for the first five innings and were threatening to shrink a two-run deficit the A's had managed to hold since the second inning.

The crowd was in a frenzy as Mike Scioscia came to the plate with a runner in scoring position and Shelby standing on first. With fans on their feet and voicing their approval, and the Oakland bullpen beginning to stir, Scioscia, batting from the left side against the right-hander Stewart, took a called strike on the outside corner of the plate, putting Stewart ahead on the count, 0-1.

Back came Stewart with a fastball that Scioscia timed perfectly, drilling it over short and on into left field. The slow-footed Marshall lumbered around third to score the Dodgers' third run of the game while Shelby held at second base. On the strength of three consecutive singles, the A's lead had been cut to one, 4-3, and the Dodgers suddenly had some life.

"The momentum changed in our favor," backup catcher Dempsey said. "We had too many good, veteran players [to ever give up.]"

Relievers Cadaret and Gene Nelson scrambled to loosen up in the A's bullpen while pitching coach Dave Duncan scurried to the mound to consult with his struggling pitcher. Convinced that the 20-game winner was still sharp enough to extricate himself from the worsening jam, Duncan turned toward the A's dugout and walked away, leaving his hurler to face third baseman Hamilton, the Dodgers' fifth batter of the inning, the number-seven hitter in the lineup, and a player who had hit just under .300 with runners in scoring position during the regular season. With Shelby and Scioscia running on the pitch, Hamilton fouled off Stewart's first service: 0-1.

Stewart came back at Hamilton with a ball inside that nearly hit him. Hamilton then fouled Stewart's third pitch to the backstop, leaving the batter behind in the count at 1-2. Finally, Hamilton smacked a pitch on the ground to third baseman Lansford, who stepped on the bag and fired across the infield to McGwire to complete an easy double play. While the Dodgers' rally had come to a sudden and, in the eyes of Oakland manager La Russa, merciful halt, the damage had been done. The home team had clawed back to within one run of the A's with three innings left to play.

Meanwhile, things were starting to happen behind the scenes.

"I went down to the clubhouse in the sixth or seventh inning, and [Gibson] was milling about," reliever Horton said. "I'd seen him earlier in the day and I can picture him wearing gym shorts with ice bags on both knees and both shoulders—he had ice bags everywhere. I couldn't imagine him taking an at-bat—it just didn't seem realistic to me."

For the next two innings, from the top of the seventh through the middle of the ninth, Game One played itself as both teams phoned in their at-bats. Holton gave up a walk to Parker in the seventh and Stewart allowed a single and a stolen base to Sax in the bottom half. Alejandro Pena came on in relief to turn the A's away in order in the eighth, and Stewart shut down the Dodgers one-two-three in the bottom half. Pena allowed an infield single to Stan Javier in the top of the ninth and nothing more before retiring the side.

"Tim [Belcher] gave up the grand slam early to Jose, but then he shut it down—he got through it and got it to the bullpen," said Cadaret, who warmed up in the A's bullpen but never saw action in Game One.

After 8-1/2 innings of play, Oakland maintained a slim 4-3 lead with the Dodgers preparing to bat in the last half of the ninth, the numbers six, seven, and eight batters—the bottom of the order—scheduled to hit. As the crowd rose to its collective feet, with the least productive Dodger hitters coming to bat, few could imagine the drama yet to come.

CHAPTER 10

THE BATBOY

We'd had season tickets since the stadium opened—my dad bought them back in 1962 and we had them up until a couple of years ago. There were four seats right behind the plate: aisle five, row R, seats one through four. That game was on my 28th birthday and my parents, my brother, and I went. Of course, it was an amazing game and a most amazing finish. I sat in seat one on the aisle, right behind actor Ken Berry.

During the ninth inning, when the Dodgers were losing 4-3, a guy wearing a full Oakland A's uniform walked up our aisle, taunting the Dodger fans. He was saying, "Eckersley's in there, there's no way you'll win, you guys are done, it's over."

We didn't know for sure that Gibson wouldn't be playing. We were hoping he would. When he didn't start, it was so disappointing, and I thought, "I don't know if we have a chance."

Where we were sitting we couldn't see Gibson until he walked into the on-deck circle in the ninth inning. The count got to 0-2, then 3-2, and he one-armed a ball into the seats. The crowd did not stop cheering for 20 minutes—it seemed like forever. Everyone was hugging someone. People were hugging total strangers and going crazy. It was amazing. We stood there for 20 or 30 minutes after the game and just watched. I can't believe the Dodgers won that World Series in five games. —Scott Dondanville, 60, Carlsbad, California

Of all the heroes involved in Game One, part-time air conditioner salesman Mitch Poole was probably the unlikeliest. He never threw a pitch, never hit a ball, never stole a base, never even threw a player out. Up until his big moment in the ninth inning he had never played a minute of baseball in either the major or minor leagues. Outside of college, Poole never enjoyed a baseball career of any kind, other than as a non-playing member of the Dodgers organization. In fact, Poole wasn't permitted inside the dugout that evening despite having a specific role with the team, so his time was largely spent in the clubhouse and trainer's room.

At age 24, Poole was a Dodger batboy, earning $25 per day helping the team in various capacities. As it turned out, he also may have been the team's secret weapon. Without the compliant Poole, Kirk Gibson might not have batted that day and he likely wouldn't have succeeded as he did at the end of Game One.

Although newspaper accounts the morning after Game One casually mentioned Poole's role in the Dodgers' eventual victory, it was largely forgotten and little was said. Until 25 years later, when an article on him appeared in a Los Angeles newspaper. Other media picked up on the story, and before long Poole was a minor celebrity, at least around Los Angeles, throwing out the first pitch at Dodger Stadium as Kirk Gibson's proxy when the team honored the slugger on Kirk Gibson Bobblehead Night in 2012. Poole was, finally, a symbolic member of the team, and as such he noted how one fellow member of the organization—manager Lasorda, who had checked on Gibson's status each inning—shooed him away from the dugout, nearly ordering away the cavalry with two out in the bottom of the ninth. Fortunately, Poole persisted—during the World Series, with Game One on the line, surrounded by highly trained coaches, Lasorda would even listen to a batboy. It's a testament to the manager's greatness.

Thomas Charles Lasorda was born in Norristown, Pennsylvania, on September 22, 1927, one of five boys reared by Italian immigrants Sabatino and Carmella Lasorda. As a teenager, Lasorda showed great promise as a southpaw pitcher, and he signed with the hometown Philadelphia

Phillies at the tender age of 18 in 1945 before leaving baseball the next year to fulfill a two-year military commitment.

Lasorda's baseball career began in Class D ball with the Concord Weavers and he failed to impress, winning three games, losing 12, and registering a 4.09 ERA. From there he moved to the Schenectady Blue Jays in 1948 [Class C], then was purchased by the Dodgers, who sent him on to the Greenville Spinners in Class A ball.

After that he made the short hop over to Montreal and Class AAA in 1950, where Lasorda remained through the 1953 season. He debuted with the Brooklyn Dodgers on August 5, 1954, finishing the season with nine innings pitched and a 5.00 ERA in four games. He did not win a game.

In fact, Lasorda never won a game for any major-league team. He eventually joined the Kansas City Athletics in 1956, going 0-4, then drifted around the minor leagues for several years until finally retiring from the game as a player in 1960. His minor-league record is impressive enough at 136-104; his major-league record is not so much: 0-4.

After retiring as a player Lasorda's star began to rise and he finally found his niche as a non-player. He worked as a Dodgers scout for five

Late afternoon view of Dodger Stadium's right-field bleachers, scene of late-inning heroics (© Steven K. Wagner).

years, then managed in the minors from 1966 through 1972. He returned to the big leagues as third-base coach for the Los Angeles Dodgers in 1973 under legendary Hall of Fame manager Walt Alston, who had managed him in 1955. When Alston retired in 1976, Lasorda was named manager of the club.

Lasorda wasted little time rising to the top as a field boss. He led the Dodgers to National League pennants in 1977 and 1978, losing to the Yankees in the World Series both times but beating them in 1981 to bring the Dodgers their fourth world championship in Los Angeles. He later led the Dodgers to a world championship in 1988.

"Guys ask me, don't I get burned out?" Lasorda once said. "How can you get burned out doing something you love?"[1]

In 21 seasons as manager of the Dodgers, Lasorda won 2,123 games, lost 1,851, recorded a .534 winning percentage, won two World Series, and managed countless Most Valuable Player and Cy Young Award winners. In 2000, with his professional career effectively over, Lasorda managed the U.S. Olympic baseball team that won a gold medal in Sydney, Australia. At that point he was ever the motivator, one of the most recognized figures in all of sports and an expert ambassador for the game he loved. He also had the memory of an elephant.

Once asked about a little-known Dodger prospect who had died in a car accident half a century earlier, Lasorda replied, without hesitating: "He was a good ballplayer. He had power, he could do everything. . . . I played against his dad."

To cap his career, Lasorda was inducted into the Baseball Hall of Fame in 1997, one year after retiring as manager of the Dodgers. It was, perhaps, his proudest moment.

"Baseball—you gotta love it," he said in his Hall of Fame induction speech at Cooperstown, New York.

"This is the greatest thing that ever happened to me in my lifetime," he told the crowd, which included luminaries Sandy Koufax, Pee Wee Reese, Sparky Anderson, and others. "[As a manager] I've been fortunate enough to win world championships, Cy Young awards, MVP [awards], nine rookies of the year, all-star games, but they come and go. The Hall of Fame is eternity, and I thank God for all of it. I am living a dream."[2]

While the bulk of Lasorda's life was positive, there were solemn moments. On July 3, 1991, his only son, Tom Jr., died of pneumonia. Five years later, in 1996, Lasorda suffered a heart attack that ultimately ushered him out of the dugout, into retirement, and away from the stress that managing created. Sixteen years after that, in 2012, Lasorda was hospitalized in New York City after suffering another heart attack. Through it all his wife, Jo—the couple were married for 70 years until he died in 2021—stood by his side.

"I miss it," Lasorda said of managing the Dodgers. "I really and truly miss it. I wanted to manage 'til I was 90. My wife went to [then-Dodgers owner Peter O'Malley] and told him how bad I felt [about not being able to manage]. He talked to me about it. I had two bosses—Peter O'Malley and my wife."

Until he died in 2021 at the age of 94, Lasorda was still enjoying his "run" as a member of the Dodger family, still keeping an office at Dodger Stadium. He had been with the club almost continuously for 72 years, and few, if any, people have remained affiliated with the same baseball organization longer than Tom Lasorda did.

"Tommy and I became very close friends," Claire said. "We always had candid discussions, but we've remained friends through the years. He's a winner."

As he sat in the Dodger dugout on October 15, 1988, Lasorda was just days away from securing his legacy as one of the great managers of all time. Not that he won more World Series titles than anyone else—that honor belongs to Casey Stengel and Joe McCarthy,[3] both with the Yankees, who each won seven; Lasorda would win two. Nor was he necessarily the shrewdest of all big-league managers—some credit La Russa as among the wisest managerial decision-makers. But when it came to big moments, like consulting with a batboy and assigning a slugger with two bad legs to pinch-hit in the World Series with two out in the bottom of the ninth inning, a slugger who eventually won the game after hitting warmup pitches thrown by the batboy, nothing and nobody exceeded that. Not Bobby Thomson's manager, Leo Durocher, nor Bill Mazeroski's manager, Danny Murtaugh, nor Carlton Fisk's manager, Darrell Johnson.

"Tommy liked to play out of the box," ex-A's pitcher and former Dodger pitching coach Honeycutt said. "He liked to create movement. I don't know the exact number, but they were successful in about 50% of their hit-and-run plays in that series."

With one out in the bottom of the eighth inning, broadcaster Vin Scully made a dramatic announcement. After looking over the cluttered Dodger dugout from top to bottom and seeing no sign of the injured Kirk Gibson, who had appeared there earlier in the game, Scully declared, "Kirk Gibson . . . will not see any action tonight, for sure."

Scully's pronouncement was not without basis. Earlier in the game, Lasorda had approached Gibson and asked, "How's your leg?" Gibson replied, "Real bad."

"I said, 'You know, a guy has a bad leg, why don't you hit a home run?" Lasorda needled. "Then you won't have to run hard."

To those in the ballpark listening on their radios, Scully's announcement was painful. If correct, and he usually was, the Dodgers would have to proceed at that critical juncture without their star attraction. Their makeshift lineup of low-production hitters would have to dig deep to get the job done, it seemed. There were no other options.

By the ninth inning Stewart was cruising along, although the veteran's outing had not been picture-perfect by any means. He had given up six hits, all but one of them a single. He had struck out five batters, most of them during the early innings. He had walked two, hit a batter, and registered one wild pitch. As the game moved into its twilight, Stewart, as he did so often, was grinding it out.

The Dodgers contrasted by using four pitchers. After Belcher exited following two rough innings, Leary had worked a solid three, holding the A's scoreless. The curveball-throwing Brian Holton followed by pitching a near-perfect two innings before the closer Pena brought his 1.91 ERA into the game in the eighth inning, retiring the A's in order and giving up a lone single in the ninth. The stage was set for the Dodgers' final opportunity of the game.

Deep in the bowels of Dodger Stadium, another scenario was playing out as Gibson lay prone on a trainer's table, a television nearby. Having mingled in the Dodger dugout earlier in the game, Gibson was icing his legs in the clubhouse when he heard Scully declare that he, the Dodgers' star, would certainly not play. The comment riled the slugger, and he abruptly sat up and shouted an expletive.[4] He then spotted the batboy Poole, who had comparatively little of significance to do with Game One winding down.

According to Poole, Gibson arose from the table and asked the young man to fetch his uniform, with the number 23 blazoned on the back. A clubhouse underling, the former junior college pitcher complied. As Gibson hurriedly dressed, he made another request of the batboy, who was sitting on a ball bucket: Gibson wanted Poole, who at one time pitched for the Pasadena City College Lancers, to toss him balls for an impromptu batting practice session. Then, he uttered five predictive words: "This could be the script."[5]

"Kirk had his civilian clothes on," Lasorda said. "I told him, 'Go on home—you can't *do* anything.' Before he left I said, 'I don't want you to go on home—I may need you to pinch-hit.' He asked, 'How am I gonna run?' I said, 'If you hit the ball out of the ballpark, you could just walk around.'"

After hearing Scully count him out, Gibson instructed Poole to inform Lasorda that he could hit. Poole, who was wearing jeans and a tee shirt and was not allowed in the dugout, called to Lasorda from across the dugout. When the manager asked what the batboy wanted, Poole was emphatic: Gibson believed he could hit.

"I was wearing cut-off shorts and a Dodger tee shirt, so I looked kind of brutal going out there," Poole said. "I was yelling at Tommy from the other end of the dugout, and he was acting like I was a gnat on his shoulder."[6]

Lasorda asked Poole to leave him alone, noting he was trying to manage the ninth inning of a World Series game. But Poole *didn't* leave the manager alone—he persisted in conveying what Gibson had told him to say.

"Mitch came over [to the dugout] and told me [Gibson] wanted to see me," Lasorda said. "I said to Mitch, 'Leave me alone, Mitch, I'm trying to get this inning's batting order straightened out. He kept telling me, 'He wants to see you, he wants to see you.' I finally said, 'Let's go, I'll see him.' When I got over there Kirk said he could pinch-hit."

Gibson picked up the story from there. "When Tommy finally came waddling over I said, 'Hit Davis eighth and I'll hit for the pitcher,'" Gibson said. "He just said, 'You stay here,' which I did for part of the time, but I had to get out there and get a feel for the environment."[7]

On that evening, Poole's batboy duties were relatively inconsequential: while the World Series drama continued on the field, his primary responsibility was to wash player uniforms. When Gibson asked for his help, Poole was busily picking up soiled towels in the team's training room. He was not permitted either inside the dugout or on the field, even after the game was over.

After donning his uniform in record time, Gibson spotted the hitting coach Hines making his way along a runway that led toward the playing field. He called to Hines, who had held the position from 1985-86 before leaving for a year and being reassigned the job again in 1988, asking if he would throw him some pitches. However, the coach responded that he was wanted in the Dodger dugout. Hines recommended Poole for the job, set a batting tee to the desired height, and instructed Poole not to allow Gibson to bend over and pick up balls. Again, Poole complied—the soiled towels would have to wait.

"From the fifth inning on, Tommy [Lasorda] had me check with Gibby every inning," Hines said. "In the fifth, sixth, and seventh innings there was nothing. I went up in the eighth inning and [Gibson] said he may have an at-bat for us in the ninth. Tommy's face lit up when I told him that. Tommy was so excited, but he told me not to let him come [into the dugout] until the very last." Lasorda didn't want the A's to know that Gibson could hit.

Hines added, "I think he took about 15 swings [with Poole]. Eight or nine of them were just awful."

As the A's batted in the ninth inning and the Dodgers hit in the bottom half, Poole placed balls on a batting tee and pitched to Gibson with immediacy. A "crack" followed by a "clang" could be heard resonating from the Dodger dugout each time Gibson drove a pitch into the batting cage.

"He couldn't even bend back over to put the ball on the tee after he hit it," Hershiser said. "All he was trying to do was find a stance so that when he swung the bat, he wouldn't fall over."[8]

After batting in the eighth inning, Stewart was removed by La Russa to start the ninth and replaced with one of the best pitchers in baseball: the hard-throwing Dennis Eckersley, a future MVP and Cy Young Award winner. Gibson was familiar with Eckersley and at his request, Poole threw to a spot where the pitcher's patented back-door slider, which begins outside the strike zone before breaking over the outside corner of the plate, might pass. The team's scouting report indicated that Eckersley threw the pitch every time he had a full count on a batter with the tying or winning run in scoring position. If Gibson were to bat, that would be one possible scenario, he reasoned.

There were other scenarios. Eckersley might mow down the Dodgers without allowing a base runner, as he did so often to other teams in the late innings, leaving Gibson stranded in the clubhouse. Or, the Dodgers might not get a runner past first base, rendering the team's scouting report moot and leaving Gibson—assuming he batted at all—guessing at what Eckersley might throw.

Dennis Lee Eckersley was born on October 3, 1954, in Oakland, California, whose hometown A's provided the platform for his most infamous pitching performance. Over 24 seasons, Eckersley achieved a reputation as a hard-throwing, no-nonsense, side-arm pitcher and a rare player who made his mark as both an exceptional starter and a great reliever. In fact, he is one of only two pitchers who have won 20 games in a season [1978] and saved 20 games in another season,[9] the latter of which he achieved nine times. Some consider Eckersley the most overpowering pitcher ever to occupy a major-league bullpen.

After attending Washington Union High School in Fremont, California, Eckersley was drafted by the Cleveland Indians in the third round, selection number 50, of the 1972 Major-League Baseball June amateur draft, joining the organization's Class A Reno affiliate while still in his teens. That first season he went an uninspiring 5-5 with a 4.80 ERA.

"It was obvious to me Eckersley would be an outstanding pitcher," said Bob Quinn, former minor league director for the Indians. "He had outstanding speed and intimidated you with a sidearm slider. But the thing that always impressed me–and I saw him pitch in the Texas League—was his makeup. He has that extra ingredient that says he will excel. Not necessarily a perfectionist, but he wants nothing but to beat you."[10]

Eckersley spent 1973 with Reno as well, then jumped to the organization's Class AA team in San Antonio, where he posted an impressive 14-3 record and 3.40 ERA. The following season, 1975, he joined the major-league Indians and recorded an even more impressive 13-7 record with a 2.60 ERA.

After two more seasons in Cleveland, the Indians let him go and Eckersley moved over to the Boston Red Sox, remaining there from 1978 through 1984. He then jumped to the Cubs, and after three seasons the big right-hander joined the A's in 1987, earning 16 saves in his inaugural campaign. Eckersley had at last found a baseball home and an assignment—that of relief pitcher—that suited both his broad skillset and his team's pressing on-field need.

"His control is so good, I would be willing to put on the gear and catch any pitch he throws with my eyes closed," said former player, coach, and manager Johnny Oates. "I know he's going to hit some part of the glove with every pitch."[11]

Eckersley pitched nine seasons for the A's, then two with the St. Louis Cardinals and a final one with his former team, the Red Sox, before calling it quits in 1998 with 197 wins, 171 losses, and 390 saves. Over the course of his career he stuck out 2,401 batters in 3,285 innings pitched, more than six strikeouts for every nine innings. Eckersley also earned one MVP Award, one Cy Young Award, and was named to six all-star teams. He was voted into the Hall of Fame in 2004—widely acknowledged as one of the greatest relief pitchers ever.

"He's the most amazing pitcher I've ever seen," said one-time Oakland teammate Ron Darling. "He has the ability to throw a strike any time he wants. Nobody else can do that. Nobody."[12]

Perhaps Eckersley's Hall of Fame plaque describes him the best: "A top pitcher early in his career who became a dominant closer," it reads. "Combined a blazing fastball and devastating slider, pinpoint control, and a deceptive sidearm delivery . . . As a starter completed 100 games and pitched a no-hitter for Cleveland in 1977."[13] The no-hitter, thrown against the California Angels, was the 200th pitched in major-league history.[14]

"I have great admiration for Dennis," Claire said. "One of the things I always wanted in a pitcher, and particularly in a relief pitcher, was control, and Eckersley had it in spades. Few pitchers in history commanded their pitches better than Dennis. He was a master at it, and his career was interesting because he had been a starter before he became a relief pitcher.

"There are very few pitchers who can pitch in the ninth inning, because they have to have both talent and, even more important, they have to have the makeup to handle a very stressful position. Dennis had both."

There would be no more no-hitters for the 33-year-old Eckersley, whose performances by then were limited to outs rather than entire games, and as he left the A's bullpen in right field headed for the playing field in the ninth inning of Game One, with Scully proclaiming "Dennis the Menace is on his way to the mound," the stage was set. The Dodger closer Pena had dispensed with the often-deadly Canseco on a strikeout and McGwire on a foul fly ball down the right-field line, and the last Oakland threat had been extinguished. Now, all eyes turned to the big Oakland reliever, MVP of the American League Championship Series, and the minimal Dodgers offense. Eckersley was a professional, Gibson was equal to Eckersley, and however things played out, a game-winning walk-off home run in the World Series was a long shot. Especially against the likes of Eckersley, whose slider was unhittable. With only an inning left to play and the team down 4-3, the Dodgers hoped to prove otherwise.

CHAPTER II

DUEL

Our good friends had season tickets, and they'd bought tickets for [Game One]. On the spur of the moment they called to say they had tickets to the World Series and they couldn't go. They asked if my husband and I wanted to buy their tickets, so we changed our plans and went to the game, thinking we'd never have an opportunity like that again. That's the only reason why we ended up there that night.

We arrived right before the game started and our seats were on the second level, about four rows up on the third-base side. Kirk Gibson was not supposed to play that day, but I, the optimist, always believed he would bat and be the hero.

We were big Dodger fans and really felt they had a chance to win the World Series. After Canseco's grand slam in the second inning, my husband wanted to leave. He figured he'd listen to the rest of the game on the car radio. I said, "No, I'm not leaving."

I had seen Gibson before the game and he was limping. He just didn't look like he could play. So when he stuck his head out of the dugout [in the ninth inning] and I realized he was indeed heading to the on-deck circle, my husband said: "He can't hit, he can't even run to the base." I said, "I don't know, but he's going to hit a home run."

When he got to the batter's box, everyone in the stands stood up. No one was seated the whole time that he was up. It was magical–I could feel my whole body tingling. I just knew he was going to hit a home run. Then, my husband said, "He can't do this, can he? Can he really do it?"

Gibson is left-handed, so he was facing us as he batted. When he got to the plate he wasn't steady, and it seemed like it took forever for him to finally hit the ball. When he hit the home run everyone was dazed—I was stunned. I really do believe that it was Gibson's energy, the momentum of the crowd, and the positive vibes in the stadium that pushed that ball out of the park. It wasn't just the effort of Gibson or the team, it took the force of the whole stadium to make it happen. When it finally did happen the entire ballpark could breathe again. It was pandemonium. Then, Gibson could hardly run around the bases. I remember telling my husband that if we went to a million more games, nothing would surpass this one.

Afterward, no one wanted to leave. I remember thinking, "What's going to happen now—is there more?" Gibson kept coming out for encores, and all of a sudden everyone in the crowd was everyone else's best friend. The entire stadium came together, and it was a moment in time that I will never forget. After a long time, we finally left. I didn't care if I never went to another baseball game again. —Kathy Buffington Willett, 68, Draper, Utah

---

As he toed the pitching rubber, the six-foot-two Eckersley had logged 45 saves during the regular season—a remarkable number for any reliever and eight of them leading to Dave Stewart wins. With half an inning left to go, the big right-hander was hoping to make it nine. The first Dodger standing in his path was the catcher Scioscia, who had singled in the sixth inning to drive in the Dodgers' third run of the game. As if to hasten the pitcher's mission toward victory, Scioscia jumped on the second pitch and lifted an Eckersley fastball to the second baseman Weiss, who caught it easily just behind second base. One away.

It was Scioscia who had turned around the National League Championship Series with a ninth-inning home run off Mets ace Dwight Gooden in a game that Kirk Gibson later won with a twelfth-inning home run.

Tom Lasorda (© Everett Raymond Kinstler, National Portrait Gallery, Smithsonian Institution).

This night was different, however, and as he trotted toward the Dodger dugout there would be no offensive drama for Scioscia. Instead, with one away Scioscia relinquished the focus to Jeff Hamilton, a 29th-round draft pick who brought a .230 career batting average to the plate against one of the great pitchers in baseball history. Clearly, the young third baseman was overmatched. Eckersley fired a fastball that Hamilton fouled off to the right side, putting him in an early hole.

As Gibson sat in the Dodger dugout, wearing a batting helmet, slipping on his batting glove, then holding a bat while seated next to Scioscia, his intentions were palpable: he expected to hit. Whether that coincided with Lasorda's strategy remained to be seen. Gibson stared at the dugout floor, contemplating the evolving scenario, as Eckersley came back at Hamilton with another fastball that the third-year player watched zoom by for a called second strike. The hole was gaping: 0-2.

That hole became a crater on the next pitch when Eckersley blew a third consecutive fastball by Hamilton for a called third strike. Suddenly, just minutes into the final half-inning of play, the Dodgers were down to their final out and Eckersley appeared in command.

In a move that reflects Lasorda's at-times impenetrable brilliance, pinch hitter Mike Davis, in his second to last season in the majors, was ordered to bat for Alfredo Griffin. Griffin had hit .199 during the regular season, and what better time to pinch-hit for him than with a World Series game on the line, Lasorda reasoned. Curiously, the manager replaced his shortstop with a player who hit less than Griffin: only .196 in 1988 and zero in the 1988 NLCS.

"I was in Lasorda's dog house," Davis said of the 1988 season, when expectations of him were high. "I was buried on the bench, getting playing time now and then when a game was out of hand. I was a born-again believer and I had been to God on my knees, praying all the time, talking [with God] about my season, which was one of the worst of my career."

He added, "I had come out of prayer and the word that I got from the Lord . . . was that I was going to hit a home run that series, and I did. I got up to the plate with two outs in the bottom of the ninth [in Game One], and everything I had heard in prayer was lining up." While the home run would not come until the final game of the World Series, Davis' appearance in Game One was one for the ages.

Michael Dwayne Davis was born in San Diego, California, on June 11, 1959. In 10 seasons as a big leaguer, eight of them with the A's, he won no appreciable awards, although he did have some fine seasons and collected 91 home runs—he hit 24 homers in 1982, 22 in 1987, and 19 in 1986. Despite those statistics, he'll always be remembered for his one

World Series at-bat against Eckersley, which did not produce a home run or even a base hit.

After graduating from Herbert Hoover High School in 1977, Davis was selected by the A's in the third round, 69th overall pick, of the 1977 June amateur draft. He spent the next three seasons playing for teams in Medicine Hat, Alberta, Canada [Rookie league]; Modesto, California [Class A]; and Waterbury, Connecticut [Class AA] before Oakland elevated him to the big club in 1980. That first season in Oakland, in 95 at-bats, he hit one home run and batted .211. The A's sent him to their Class AAA team in Tacoma, Washington, for some work.

Davis returned briefly to the A's in 1981 and 1982 before catching on for good in 1983, hitting a respectable eight home runs and driving in 62 runs while hitting .275. Four years later he caught the eye of new Dodgers general manager Fred Claire, who signed him in a two-year contract worth $2 million prior to the 1988 season. His cumulative batting average at the time was .267.

After that, Davis struggled, hitting two home runs with 17 RBI in 1988 and five home runs with 19 RBI in an injury-plagued 1989 season, his final year in the major leagues. Two seasons of minor league ball followed, then Davis retired from baseball.

On the season, Davis' worst since he broke in with the A's in 1980, the one-time third-round draft pick had punched out 55 hits, including 11 doubles, two triples, two home runs, and 17 RBI. Facing the great Eckersley with a season-long history of struggling against National League pitchers, the deck was stacked against the 29-year-old Southern California native.

Davis batted from the left side, so it made sense to insert him against the right-hander Eckersley. But why not Gibson, who also batted left-handed? Historians will attribute Lasorda's decision to genius. Or perhaps stupidity. Or providence. Or something else outside the realm of baseball logic. Whatever the reason, the strategy to bat Davis paid off—if it hadn't, Lasorda would have been fodder for relentless news media criticism—"I look like a genius, or I look like a nut," as he eloquently put it.

"[The media] had a good shot at me for pitching Hershiser" in relief to win Game Four of the NLCS just one day after he started Game Three, Lasorda said. "Nobody ever thought I'd bring him in for relief, but we ran out of pitchers."

However Davis's insertion as a pinch hitter came about, statistically speaking the clash with Eckersley was a Davis-versus-Goliath matchup. Davis kicked at the dirt several times with his right foot as he stepped into the batter's box before finally getting comfortable, the crowd becoming increasingly restless as the game neared an apparent conclusion. Through bug-eyed goggles, Davis, hitting .167 as a pinch hitter, stared out at the dominant Eckersley, who greeted him with a fastball that Davis fouled out of play: 0-1.

Eckersley followed with a slider that drifted outside, then another. And another. With the count 3-1, the crowd sensed a possible turnabout. Finally, just two strikes from victory, Eckersley blazed a fourth consecutive slider that spun outside for ball four, and Davis trotted down to first base with a walk.

"I just lost him," Eckersley said. "I shouldn't have walked him. Mike could run a little bit, too, so I knew they were going to mess around there. [Dave] Anderson was on deck, but he wasn't even on my mind."[1]

Added A's first base coach Lachemann: "When Davis walked, putting the tying run on base, that was big because Eckersley was slow to the plate and they could run on him.

"Eck didn't walk *anybody*."

The Dodgers were clinging to life with the tying run on first and the winning run, represented by whomever Lasorda chose to ordain, coming to the plate. Standing on deck was Dave Anderson, a .249 hitter with only two home runs on the season. Anderson, a pinch-hit decoy whose presence forced Eckersley to pitch around the home run hitter Davis, would not bat.

"After Davis got on, Eck probably figured Anderson doesn't have a chance against me," Lasorda said. "That's when he got the surprise of his life. Anderson didn't walk [into] that batter's box. Gibson did."[2]

Like a bobber dancing on the surface of a pond, Gibson's head popped above the dugout roof as he scrambled up the few steps leading from the hard concrete floor to the playing field, the cheers and consternation of 56,000 fans rising with each labored step. Beyond the massive parking lot the hills were dark, but inside Dodger Stadium a ray of hope glimmered. Only a faint glow, perhaps, but bright enough to feed the passion. Gibson, the man whom Vin Scully had proclaimed "for sure" would not play, in fact *would*. If only for a moment, as a pinch-hitter, for Dave Anderson or Alejandro Pena, depending upon your perspective. At that instant, there was little perspective—or clarity. *Gibson would bat*, laying to rest the word transposition that had lingered for 8-1/2 long innings: *would Gibson bat?* The next question was: if the team leader all season long was physically unable to play earlier, to push off his painful left leg to stride into a pitch and land on his painful right leg, why was Lasorda inserting Gibson at a critical moment with Game One of the World Series on the line? Was this a desperation move, a last resort? And if Gibson *could* bat, with what effectiveness? Fifty percent? Twenty-five percent? Ten percent?

As he exited the dugout Gibson appeared focused and deliberate, stopping near the on-deck circle to wipe down his bat with pine tar before executing several practice swings. He waved the bat again and again as the crowd stood on its feet and roared.

"He kind of jumped out of the dugout," the hitting coach Hines said, adding that he was surprised Gibson was physically able to depart the dugout with so much energy. "The adrenaline in him was sky high, and I believe he did things at that moment that he could never have done an hour ahead of that or an hour after that."

In the Dodger bullpen, situated along the left-field line, the pitchers were stunned.

"I was sitting next to Jay Howell and Jessie Orosco, and when [Gibson] came out of the dugout, our group reaction was, 'What in the world is Tommy [Lasorda] doing? This doesn't make any sense, because he can't even stand up,'" reliever Horton said. "As teammates, we did not think it was physically possible for him to take an at-bat."

To Eckersley, Gibson's ascent from the dugout was a dream come true. Or perhaps a nightmare. A dream come true if indeed Gibson was so injured that he couldn't and shouldn't hit. A nightmare if he really *was* well enough to affect the outcome of a game that the A's led by so narrow a strand. Either way, the die was cast and Gibson would bat. Eckersley would throw.

"Why would Lasorda choose to pinch-hit with a guy who was half disabled in a critical moment against one of the greatest closers that baseball has ever seen?" wondered former Dodger ace Erskine, author of two no-hitters, winner of two World Series games, and witness to Bobby Thomson's famous home run. "You put those things together and you say, 'No—it's fiction.' But you know the old saying—'life is stranger than fiction.' He added, "Why would Lasorda choose the guy who was least likely to be able to walk to the plate?"

Over in the A's dugout, La Russa sat calmly, scorecard resting on his lap. At this late juncture, his scorecard meant little. Eckersley, the best the A's had, would pitch. Gibson, the best the Dodgers had, at least when healthy, would bat. There was no equivocation. There were no names to cross out. There were no more decoys standing in the on-deck circle. If Gibson made out, the game would be over. If he doubled or better, the game would likely be tied and the top of the Dodgers order would be coming up. Nothing would interrupt the Eckersley-versus-Gibson duel now—it was two out, bottom of the ninth.

Standing in the batter's box, the man who endured pain with each step just to get there was perhaps the best athlete on the field. Kirk Harold Gibson was born in Pontiac, Michigan, on May 28, 1957, the youngest child of Bob and Barbara Gibson. His father taught math at Kettering High School, which young Kirk attended through graduation, and his mother taught speech and theater at another local high school.

As a boy, Gibson admittedly was spoiled. "My parents never made me work," he said. "When I grew up, all we did was screw around with motorcycles and water-ski. I had it pretty easy." However, "My dad pushed me hard in athletics. He built me a home plate and mound in the backyard and a [basketball] hoop over the garage, and he made me practice."[3]

So much that Gibson developed the mental toughness and discipline needed to excel, traits that would serve him well later on. Excel he did, even as a youth, leading his American Legion team to a state championship in 1975; he hit a home run, the first of many big blasts to come, that propelled his team to the title game.

Gibson had also excelled at football, his primary athletic interest, and he eventually enrolled at Michigan State University after the program offered him a scholarship to play for the Spartans. Starting at flanker as a freshman, Gibson scored his first touchdown in his second collegiate game and caught four touchdown passes on the season, including one for 82 yards. The next season, playing under legendary coach Darryl Rogers, Gibson caught 39 passes for 748 yards and led everyone in the Big 10 Conference in pass receiving.

Following his successful junior season, Gibson was asked by the MSU baseball coach to consider playing that sport as well. He agreed to do so and flourished, hitting .390 with 16 home runs and 52 RBI in his only season of college baseball. Gibson made all-American and his sights began to shift from football to baseball.

When the 1978 major-league baseball June amateur draft rolled around, Gibson was high on the lists of several teams, and he was selected 12th in the first round by his hometown Detroit Tigers. He signed a six-year contract worth $200,000 and reported to the team's Class A Lakeland Flying Tigers in 1978, where his numbers that first year were acceptable: eight home runs, 40 RBI, and a .240 batting average, acceptable considering he only logged 175 at-bats.

Detroit had high hopes for the six-foot-three, 215-pound outfielder, and the following season the Tigers briefly called him up to the big leagues—he made his major-league debut on September 8, 1979, and hit his first home run two weeks later. In 38 at-bats that year he collected nine hits, including three doubles, one home run, and four RBI. He hit .237.

The following season the Tigers sent Gibson down to the Class AA Evansville Triplets. On the strength of 327 at-bats he had one of his worst seasons, his best being 1985 when he hit 29 home runs and knocked in 97 runners. Three years later he signed as a free agent with the Dodgers.

In 17 seasons with four major-league clubs Gibson slugged 255 home runs, knocked in 870 runners, and recorded a lifetime batting average of .268. He ranks 79th overall for career strikeouts by a major-league hitter with 1,285[4] and is the only former MVP to never play in an all-star game.

For 20 long seconds, Gibson dug his left foot into the soft dirt near home plate, back and forth, repeatedly scratching to get a foothold, then stepped away as if to declare "not yet." He gazed briefly toward Eckersley, then shot a glance at first-base coach Manny Mota, took a practice swing, and repositioned himself back inside the batter's box. Eckersley, perspiring slightly, caught a sign from Oakland's new catcher Ron Hassey, then straddled the rubber to deliver his first pitch: fastball, fouled back, 0-1.

Gibson stepped back again, circled around, tapped both cleats with his black-barreled bat, and swung back into position to await the next pitch. After Eckersley fired a pickoff throw in hopes of catching Davis meandering too far off first base, the pitcher came back with another fastball that Gibson again fouled back, 0-2. Gibson and the Dodgers were down to their final strike in a game that few believed they would win.

Still, they had played the A's close into the ninth inning and were losing by only a run, although time was short. With Game One at stake, Gibson breathed deeply and Eckersley made two more throws to his first baseman McGwire in an effort to hold Davis on, then delivered another fastball that Gibson dribbled slowly toward first.

"I remember hitting the little dribbler down the line, and it wasn't pretty," Gibson said.[5]

As he hobbled down the line the pain in Gibson's legs was evident. However, McGwire and Eckersley converged on the ball, with McGwire fielding it inches into foul territory, enabling Gibson to rest his battered wheels as he made his way back toward home plate. Davis returned to the bag and the count remained at 0-2.

"It was terrible," Hershiser said. "Just terrible. We were in the dugout thinking he shouldn't have even tried to hit."

Eckersley agreed. "He looked so feeble," he said. "I thought I was going to blow him away. I thought he was a lamb. I'm thinking, 'I'm going to throw him a high fastball and he's done.'"[6]

If anything, Gibson's painful sprint confirmed one thing to Lasorda: with his hitter's extremities in obvious pain, preventing him from stepping forcefully into a swing, it was not likely he would hit a home run. Also disconcerting, if he hit a ball on the ground there was little chance Gibson would beat a throw to first—the game would end right there. Lasorda wanted Davis on second base so that any batted ball that kissed the outfield grass might score a run and tie the game.

As Gibson walked slowly back toward the catcher Hassey, Eckersley returned to the pitching rubber and delicately toed it. He, too, had made a dash on the play, and whether that would affect his momentum was uncertain. Unlike Gibson, Eckersley's legs were both healthy. However, any added exertion—such as running hard to field a ball—could affect his pitching rhythm.

With a single tap to each cleat, Gibson stepped back in to face his opponent. Eckersley, hunched slightly at the shoulders, straightened into his stretch again and unloaded. A fastball slithered outside for a ball and Hassey jumped from his crouch and fired a shot to first, nearly catching Davis leaning toward second. Davis dived safely back into the bag: 1-2.

Eckersley's next pitch, his 15th consecutive fastball, was fouled into the seats behind the Dodger dugout as Davis took off for second on a steal attempt. The count remained 1-2.

"Eckersley got two strikes on him and it was terrible the way he was swinging," Lasorda said.

The scene had become predictable. With each pitch, Gibson stepped back from the batter's box, tapped his cleats, moved back in, and dug his spikes into the loose, powdery dirt. He completed a few practice swings, then fixed his stance in the box. While he did this, Eckersley alternately stared down toward Hassey for a sign and glanced at Davis on first before delivering. Like the four balls that missed the strike zone and sent Davis scurrying to first with a walk, Eckersley's next pitch also broke outside, and the count to Gibson was even at 2-2.

Eckersley stretched and again fired quickly to first, with Davis diving back to the bag once more. On the next pitch, which curled outside for ball three, Davis broke for second and stole the base without a throw.

"I wouldn't have sent Mike down on the first pitch because then they would have had the opportunity to walk [Gibson]," Lasorda said. "I knew Eckersley was a great relief pitcher and he wouldn't walk anybody. When we got two strikes on Gibson we decided to put the steal sign on and get in position to tie the game. At that point I was thinking about [Gibson getting] a base hit and tying the game. It didn't work out that way. Unfortunately for Oakland, something dropped from Heaven."

Intentionally or not, as Davis arrived at second, Gibson's body swung toward the plate and blocked Hassey from firing toward the base. The Dodgers had the tying run in scoring position with a full count on Gibson.

"With Dennis Eckersley's high leg kick I knew I could steal second base," Davis said. "I *asked* to [steal]." Davis did so knowing that "if I get picked off or if I get thrown out trying to steal, they might as well just dig a hole and bury me. I'd be mincemeat forever in L.A."

Dempsey, who spent 24 years as a major-league catcher before retiring after the 1992 season, laughed. "It was part of the package," he said. "Working that count and getting a walk was incredible. Then, stealing second base—[Davis] was just the right guy at the right time."

The stolen base also created pressure for the third-base coach Amalfitano, who might have to decide whether to send Davis home should Gibson get a hit. He denies there was any additional pressure on him.

Following Davis's successful steal, Gibson turned his back on home plate and walked several paces toward the Oakland dugout, perhaps to collect his thoughts as the crowd roared with excitement. He turned back around, tapped his right cleat, and returned to his position near the plate. The drama was unambiguous: two out, bottom of the ninth, full count, tying run on second, Oakland leading 4-3. The American League's toughest pitcher was facing the National League's toughest hitter, and on deck was the second baseman Sax, who already had a single in the game. Sax would not hit.

Inside the A's dugout La Russa fidgeted, perhaps hoping his fidgeting would magically change the game's trajectory. Gibson pointed his bat toward the pitcher as Eckersley went into his stretch. Eckersley stared down toward Hassey, hands together at his waist, then Gibson held his hand up to signal time out, backpedaling off the plate. He took a deep breath.

"All of a sudden he called time out and got off to the side where he could probably think about 'What am I gonna do?'" Lasorda said.

Dodgers third-base coach Joe Amalfitano, who spoke with Gibson the following day, said Lasorda's assessment was correct. "I asked him, 'Why did you back out?' He said, 'I was collecting my thoughts.'"

Davis, looking on from second base, perceived it the same way. "Kirk did a great job stepping out and getting refocused."

At some point during the at-bat Gibson says he smiled as Dodger scout Mel Didier's comments rang in his head. With two strikes, Gibson knew what pitch was coming.

Eckersley had scarcely moved from his stretch position as Gibson re-entered the box, repeated his gestures, steadied himself, and waited for the next pitch—the final pitch of the game.

After six long minutes of gamesmanship, the duel had reached a denouement. With most of the 54,000 fans standing and screaming, Gibson recollected the scouting report on Eckersley, authored by Didier, who died in 2017: with the tying or winning run in scoring position and a full count on the batter, the Oakland pitcher always threw a back-door slider. *Always.*

"Podnuh, let me tell you this," Didier drawled at the Dodgers left-handed hitters. "If Eckersley gets you at 3-2 and there's a runner at second base or third base, and it's the tying or winning run, Eckersley will throw you a back-door slider on 3-2. Don't forget that because that's what he will do as sure as I'm standing here breathing."[7]

Gibson was counting on that as Eckersley went into his stretch before delivering the next pitch, his final one of the ballgame.

"When it got to a 3-2 count I thought about Mel Didier," Gibson said. "I stepped out and told myself, 'Partner, sure as I'm standing here breathing, you're going to see a 3-2 back-door slider.'"[8]

A's coach Lachemann said Didier's scouting report wasn't completely accurate, that Eckersley didn't always throw the back-door slider in key situations. "He had command of other pitches. It depended on what the situation was," Lachemann said. "He'd mix it up. If he threw that pitch every single time in those situations, word would get around. That's not the case."

With two out and a full count, Davis broke quickly on the pitch. As the ball sailed toward home plate Gibson, whose injured left leg precluded him from striding into the ball with authority, used his powerful arms to muscle a back-door slider that arced on a low trajectory toward the right-field fence. At that moment the only man standing between Gibson and a Dodger victory was the right fielder Canseco, whose second-inning home run was the difference in the ballgame. Like a cat, Canseco moved to his left.

CHAPTER 12

THE SHOT – 5-4

I always sat near the steps leading from the dugout onto the field in case I wanted to tell the guys something [as they went to bat], maybe a pitch to look for—but mostly to pat them on the rear and say, "Go get 'em, Tiger." Kirk had been in the trainer's room lounging around, and he kept hearing [Vin Scully] say he would be a no-show for the entire game. That made him mad— you can't tell Gibby he can't do this or he can't do that.

Kirk jumped out of the dugout when his spot came up to hit, and there was such a roar from the stands when he showed up in the on-deck circle. The adrenaline in him was sky high, and I believe he did things at that moment that he could never have done an hour ahead of that or an hour after that. The adrenaline of the moment got inside him—Kirk had played football, and it was like a football player being told he couldn't play, then he gets in the game at the very end, it's close, and he can make a difference.

He never did get his hips into the home run—that was all wrist and hands. You can't do what he did against the best pitcher in baseball, but his football mentality was telling him he could. I didn't expect it to be a home run until I saw it land in the stands. When he first hit it I thought, "That thing's got a chance to be off the wall for extra bases, but I don't know if Gibby can get to second." It really caught the right fielder flat-footed. I think it caught 99 percent of the world flat-footed. At that point, I was as much of a fan as anybody in the stadium—I was yelling and hoopin' and hollerin'. I can't even remember getting out of the dugout and going over to home plate. But before I knew it I was there in a crowd. Watching him go around the bases was so exciting. —Ben Hines, the former Dodgers hitting coach who died in 2021

With echoes of Brooklyn left fielder Andy Pafko watching helplessly as Bobby Thomson's memorable home run soared out of the Polo Grounds to break the Dodgers' hearts, Canseco took several obligatory strides, looked over his shoulder, then watched the ball crash into a sea of screaming fans. The explosion meant only one thing.

"I was watching Canseco, and his body language indicated to me that we had just won the game," coach Amalfitano said.

Across the field, Eckersley, wide-eyed after giving up only his sixth home run all year, watched the ball's flight in horror. In marked contrast, Lasorda raised his hands above his head and leaped for joy, running onto the field along with the entire Dodger team. La Russa was stunned and his A's, demoralized over the abrupt metastases—their demoralization would carry through the entire Series—walked off the field into a visitors clubhouse where, fittingly, the power would soon go out.

"I didn't look," said Laurie Lachemann, wife of A's first-base coach Rene Lachemann, who was seated with the other wives in a designated section behind home plate. "I turned my head. I'm not sure I could watch it today."

Suddenly, in the blink of an eye, in the time it takes to swing a bat and watch its swift flight exceed a far-off blue barrier, the game was over and the Dodgers had won. As he always did, Scully made the call with impeccable style, the words rolling off his tongue with fluidity: "High fly ball into right field, she is gone!" he said. Scully said nothing for the 68 seconds that followed, allowing the roar of the crowd and the words he had already spoken to sink in and do his talking. Scully then continued: "In a year that has been so improbable, the impossible has happened."

Improbable, too, was Lasorda's decision to send a badly injured Gibson to the plate. If Gibson had failed, Lasorda would have received withering criticism.

Kirk Gibson at Michigan State University (courtesy of Michigan State University Athletic Communications).

"Believe me, Tommy wasn't worried about that whatsoever," Claire said. "That's what made Tommy the Hall of Fame manager that he was. He went with his heart, he went with his instincts, and [not batting

Gibson] was not even a consideration. Kirk can bat? You bet. That's who Tommy is. That's who Kirk is."

As gleeful fans scrambled to retrieve Gibson's home run ball—the successful recipient has never come forward—thus began the slowest home run trot in major-league history. His injuries were clearly painful, and it so pained those watching him that many observers wondered whether Gibson would even finish his trek around the bases. He did. As the ball tumbled among delighted fans, nothing would keep Gibson, whose injuries were so debilitating that he was excused from pre-game introductions, from circumnavigating the baseball diamond. He was, certainly, the man of the hour—it would be his only hour, his only six minutes, actually, during the World Series. Those six minutes going nose to nose with Eckersley were the only minutes he would play. They were six minutes that changed the organization's disposition.

"The story is Michael Davis," said Eckersley. "I walked him. I don't walk *anybody!* I gave him too much credit. I had played with Michael the year before, and he hit over 20 home runs with us. I gave him way too much credit . . . In my mind, I wasn't facing the guy who was hitting under .200 for the Dodgers. That's where it all goes wrong."

Davis echoed that assessment. "Eckersley probably remembered me from when I played with Oakland [in 1987]—I got a lot of big hits for the A's," Davis said. "He didn't realize that I had struggled during my first year with the Dodgers. He was remembering me from when I was his teammate, and he didn't go too deep into the stat book to see how bad I was in 1988."

In Lasorda's mind, Davis' at-bat and his steal of second were crucial.

"If Mike hadn't got on base, Gibson wouldn't have hit," he said. "Mike Davis was a talented player."

From the second he made contact, Gibson knew the ball would clear the right-field fence. Others, including Davis, weren't so sure. As he rounded third base, "I probably took a peek," Davis laughed. The ball traveled four rows deep into the bleachers, not a long home run by Dodger Stadium standards. Gibson paused to watch its flight as he understood that something extraordinary might be happening. Something huge. Something cataclysmic, as indeed the ground beneath Dodger Stadium shook when the thunderous ovation rumbled with the vengeance of a San Andreas temblor.

"I told myself when I stepped out onto the field that the ovation and the environment would be outstanding and I wouldn't hurt anymore, and it was true," Gibson said. "I didn't stay in the on-deck circle very long. I just walked up there.

"It was like the movie *The Natural*. It was very similar."[1]

Bill Virdon, 1955 National League Rookie of the Year, a former major-league manager, and witness to Mazeroski's memorable 1960 World Series blast, was more philosophical. "That's baseball," he said. "You never know what's going to happen. You can bat the best [hitter] against the worst [pitcher] and nothing will happen. You can bat the worst [hitter] against the best [pitcher] and he'll hit a home run. It happens."

Fans reacted to the drive with immediacy. As Gibson paused briefly, eyes trained on the ball as it exploded off his bat, the roar began. With his arm raised in triumph, Gibson limped to first base at half speed, robotically rounded the bag, waved his right arm in a circular forward motion, and hoped he had the physicality to reach second. He dutifully touched second base with both arms raised in jubilation, turned the corner again, and performed a double fist pump. Gibson nervously tipped his helmet in the direction of fans behind the Dodger dugout and continued on in hopes of completing the formality of touching all four bases. Whether he would succeed was not a sure thing, at least to those observing.

Gibson rounded the final bag and smacked the right hand of third-base coach Amalfitano, whose mouth was open wide with excitement as he danced down the line with his laboring subaltern. According to Amalfitano, who still possesses Didier's scouting report on Eckersley, a gleeful Gibson uttered four words as he rounded the bag and headed toward home: "Back-door slider, Joe!"

He then continued toward home plate, where teammates were waiting to mob him; among the first to greet Gibson were Hershiser, Sax, and the pitching coach Perranoski. He then touched the plate and disappeared into an army of exultant teammates.

One pitcher who didn't mind not pitching in that spot was Oakland reliever Greg Cadaret, who would make three appearances in the Series without giving up a run. "It wouldn't have been much fun if *I'd* given up that home run," he said, laughing. "Dennis was the best closer in baseball, that was his job, and he did it all year long."

Not that time. How did Hines, who was seated near the front steps of the Dodger dugout, react when he saw the ball exit Eckersley's hand, strike Gibson's bat, and drop into the stands? "Complete ecstasy," he said. Hines added that he believes Gibson's home run was bigger than those hit by either Thomson or Mazeroski.

Moments after the home run, Gibson returned to the field for an interview with Bob Costas, who asked him about the injury and the home run.

> I was very disappointed because I knew I couldn't play. I knew I'd be a detriment. I got an injection today and I'm very sore. But I saw the opportunity, I knew that if we could get a guy on base [that] the pitcher was coming up. I figured if I got out there and the fans started cheering, that I could suck it up for one [at-bat] and maybe something good would happen, and it happened. It was tough pushing off my front foot. My other hamstring was hurting me. I have two bad legs, but when I got two strikes on I just decided to buckle it down. [When] Mike [Davis] got to second I knew I really didn't have to hit a home run—I was going to shorten up and try to drive the ball the other way. I got a low breaking ball, the ball I like to hit, and I was just fortunate. The good Lord gave me this wonderful moment. I had a pretty good idea [that the ball was a home run the instant I hit it]. We've had some tough times, but what a team. We've been saying it all year, but if it weren't for my teammates I wouldn't have even got this opportunity to remember this moment. I had been in the trainer room all night getting treatment. In fact, I heard Vin Scully say they were panning the dugout looking

for me, [that] it didn't look like I was going to be able to play. I said, "That's enough." [I] . . . put an ice bag on, numbed my knee up as best I could, hit some off the tee in there, and I had a batboy ask Tommy [Lasorda] to come in—I wanted to talk to him. I said, "Go ahead and pinch hit for Alfredo [Griffin] with Mike [Davis]. If we get a guy on, I'll go ahead and give you my best. I think I can do it and give you a good shot." That's what it's all about. I just kept telling myself that these are the types of circumstances you enjoy most, and you perform even better under these conditions. Thank the good Lord, it all happened for us.

As the crowd's thunderous roar continued, Claire was scurrying to leave the ballpark. He was seated in a private box high above home plate when Gibson completed his *perficiendi*, but following the game-ending blast Claire quietly made his way toward his office on the Club Level, retrieved his briefcase, then wasted little time exiting the premises headed for his home in nearby Pasadena. The man who had welcomed Gibson to Los Angeles, signed him to a three-year contract, paid him handsomely—$4.5 million—then watched as he dismantled the A's with one improbable wave of the bat, left his perch before the post-game celebration he had worked tirelessly to ensure even began. For Claire, standing in a strangely quiet Dodger Stadium parking lot, the night was over.

"There was nothing more I could do," Claire said. "Kirk didn't need another slap on the back."

As a coach, Amalfitano's exit from the field wasn't as swift as Claire's, although he did manage to find time alone to reflect upon what he had witnessed. "I went upstairs to my locker and got emotional," he said. "I cried."

Lost in the shuffle, at least momentarily, was Davis, whose steal of second base forced Eckersley to throw the back-door slider that Gibson was waiting for, a pitch that Gibson knew Eckersley always threw with the tying run in scoring position and a full count on the batter.

"It was great to see Mike's [Davis] contribution there, because he'd had a difficult season," Claire said. "Mike was a guy who took responsibility. He had some really solid seasons with Oakland, and I think the

Kirk Gibson as a Michigan State Spartan (courtesy of Michigan State University Athletic Communications).

walk that Mike Davis drew from Eckersley was very much a result of Eckersley pitching to a Mike Davis who he saw make a great contribution to the Oakland club."

Relief pitcher Cadaret was still seated in the Oakland bullpen when Gibson hit the home run. The ball, he said, sailed "right over my head."

"The place got so loud that you couldn't even talk to the guy next to you," he said. "It was a surreal moment. That roar was one of the greatest moments of all time, at least for Dodger fans. When we went into the locker room it was still like that—the noise was so loud, then the power went out." For Oakland, it was literally lights out.

At least emotionally, the darkness was short-lived, according to Honeycutt. "We reflected on the game for maybe 10 or 15 minutes after we got into the clubhouse, then we moved on to prepare for the next game," he said.

Dempsey, who as a longtime American League catcher was familiar with Eckersley, put the home run pitch into perspective. "Eckersley didn't really read Gibson very well. [Gibson] could not get around on the fastball, but he had just enough to get around on that slider. It was a very defensive swing, but he was so strong that he was able to hit the ball out of that ballpark."

Afterward, Gibson was named "Player of the Game" ahead of A's right fielder Canseco, whose second-inning grand slam had set the tone for the game and who had watched helplessly as Gibson's drive cleared the right-field fence. The honor came just six days after Gibson had homered in the twelfth inning to give the Dodgers a dramatic, come-from-behind, 5-4 win over the Mets in Game Four of the National League Championship Series. Four years earlier, Gibson had homered late in Game Five of the 1984 World Series to ice that contest and the Series for Detroit; that home run was his second of the game. He had also homered in the 1984 American League Championship Series and was later named MVP for that series.

In all, Gibson hit six post-season home runs during his long career—three of them in World Series competition. None was bigger than the one he hit in Game One of the 1988 World Series, which author Josh Suchon described as ". . . the most dramatic home run in baseball history . . ."[2] *Life and News* magazine dubbed it the most famous home run ever hit in World Series play, while La Russa said there has never been a more dramatic moment in baseball given all of the circumstances.

Seated just feet from where the ball landed near the A's bullpen was reliever Honeycutt, who had a perfect view of the shot and knew at once that Gibson had hit the ball out. "As good [a view] as you can have," laughed Honeycutt, who did not allow a run in three 1988 World Series appearances. "The trajectory was just right. He squared it up really well."

Pat Kuehner is well familiar with dramatic moments in big games and walk-off hits. Playing for USC in the final game of the 1968 College World Series, Kuehner was called upon to pinch-hit with his team trailing by a run, two men on base, and two out in the bottom of the ninth inning. Although his brother had died just days before the Series began and Kuehner was hitless in 14 at-bats, he tripled off the top of the wall to drive in both runners and win the game and the national championship.

He, like Gibson, had received a scouting report predicting what the opposing pitcher would throw in his particular situation. The pitcher, like Eckersley, threw sidearm.

"That had to be one of the greatest at-bats . . . in baseball history," Kuehner, who like Gibson suffers from Parkinson's disease, said of Gibson's home run. "The whole scenario and the way it played out was just amazing. They beat Oakland's best relief pitcher, the best reliever in baseball at the time, and it had to be very demoralizing."

Kuehner added, "Because of [Gibson's] injuries, watching him swing, and watching him run the bases—with the physical considerations, that had to be *the* best or one of *the best* home runs in the history of baseball."

The following morning, on October 16, newspaper headlines across the country screamed the news: "Gibson Crashes Athletics' Victory Party," wrote the *New York Times*.[3] "Gibson's Shot in the Dark Stuns A's," added the *Los Angeles Times*.[4] "Gibson's Big Blast Jolts A's," chimed in the *Chicago Tribune*.[5]

In one memorable moment, on the greatest baseball stage of all, Gibson did all of that: he had stunned, he had jolted, he had won, and no one should have been surprised. Except, perhaps, the many faithful who had allowed themselves—understandably—to become dispirited during the 8-2/3 innings before Gibson came to bat. To them, and to those with their tail lights on beyond the outfield pavilion, Game One was kaput. Hope was lost. The joy was gone from Mudville. Wait 'til next year.

Except for one thing: Gibson had also done the improbable just six days before against the Mets. And 13 years earlier in the American Legion state tournament. Gibson was a big-game player, the World Series was baseball's top prize, and he did what the Dodgers expected when they acquired his services following the 1987 season—especially during the World Series.

Now, with Game One in the bank, the dispirited fans were once again spirited—and so were the Dodgers.

"Game One was a huge motivational change," Honeycutt said. "It was a huge lift for them, obviously a negative for us.

"You don't expect Game One to change a series. I still don't think Game One was the determining factor."

Instead of heading into Game Two down 1-0, they shut out the A's 6-0 the following night behind the three-hit pitching of Orel Hershiser, who threw a complete game. Marshall homered for the Dodgers. Gibson did not play.

The Series shifted to Oakland for Game Three and the A's pulled out a narrow 2-1 victory on the strength of McGwire's ninth-inning solo home run. Oakland accumulated only five hits in the game. Gibson did not play.

Oakland also hosted Game Four and the Dodgers won 4-3. In that game, Belcher redeemed himself for his Game One shortcomings and pitched 6-2/3 superb innings, striking out seven. Gibson did not play.

Leading in the Series 3-1, the Dodgers returned home for Game Five. Orel Hershiser, who had led the team all year long, started on the mound and pitched a four-hit, complete game, 5-2 victory. Homering for Los Angeles were Mickey Hatcher, who had hit a home run in Game One, and Mike Davis, the man who predicted he would homer and who made Kirk Gibson's dramatic home run possible by walking with two out in the ninth inning. Once again, Gibson did not play—as Scully might have said, the Dodgers once again had done the impossible.

"We still talk about it, not so much that we lost to the Dodgers, but we really felt we should have won the World Series," Carney Lansford said. "We felt like [we were the better team], but how you play in the World Series has nothing to do with how you played during the regular season."

Mike Cameron, one of 18 players to hit four home runs in a major-league game, said Gibson's home run definitely motivated his teammates going forward, "giving the Dodgers a boost of energy and excitement." However, he stopped short of saying it spelled doom for the A's in the Series. "As far as Oakland being shut down, that was due to good pitching by the Dodgers. That happens sometimes, it just goes to show you can't take any team for granted."

Over the years, as anniversaries of Gibson's home run have come and gone, players have recollected the event with more clarity than perhaps they had at the time it occurred. Most remember it with stunning detail.

Eckersley said that after the game, "I was still in shock," adding, "I was actually lucky to be where I was at the moment. I had only been closing for a year and a half, and . . . I had gone through [alcoholism] recovery. I was a different person, and I was grateful to be where I was at that time."

Said La Russa: "I don't think there's ever been a more dramatic moment in baseball because of the circumstances. That being said, whenever I see it shown I look away . . . I will not look at it . . . I've seen it too many times. Enough is enough."

Said Scully, who spent 66 years with the Dodgers organization: "Years later, I told [Gibson] . . . 'My greatest single contribution to the Dodgers was getting you off that training table.'"

Gibson recalled watching a replay of the home run and seeing cars exiting the parking lot early as his shot landed in the stands. As former Dodger Don Drysdale made the call to his radio listeners, everyone hit their brake lights simultaneously. "What [were] they going to do—stop and come back?" Gibson asked rhetorically.[6]

Said Gibson, who went on to manage in the big leagues: "It's a good story. It doesn't make sense, to be quite honest with you. . . . As manager, my motivation is to get back to that moment for somebody and to have them prepared for that moment and find their place in baseball history . . . Something tells me I will be a part of some moment again. I just feel it."[7]

He's still waiting—moments like his don't come along very often, perhaps once in a lifetime, if that. Home runs like the one Gibson hit are the intersection of skill, luck, and good timing, each converging simultaneously with the best possible result. When they do happen, they're irreplaceable, impeccable, and irretrievable. Were he alive today, Bobby Thomson might say that Gibson's home run "may have been the best thing that ever happened to anybody."[8]

AFTERWORD

I was sitting [in the Dodger bullpen] next to Jay Howell and Jessie Orosco, and when [Gibson] came out of the dugout, our group reaction was, "What in the world is Tommy [Lasorda] doing? This doesn't make any sense, because he can't even stand up." As teammates, we did not think it was physically possible for him to take an at-bat.

When we could tell that [Gibson had] hit a home run, Jesse lifted me into the air, kind of bear-hugging me around my knees or thighs. He lifted me way above him and started running around the bullpen with me in his arms. I don't know why he did that—I'd only known him for a month, for goodness sake. I remember Jesse carrying me around the bullpen and thinking we're both going to fall on the ground and get hurt. It was such a moment of elation, and he just did the first thing that came to his mind: he picked me up and carried me around.

I was in the left-field bullpen, and Gibby's home run went to right field. I'm thankful for the view I had, and it was a pretty amazing moment.

[The home run] wasn't a Game Seven winner, but it changed the Series, it was [Gibson's] only at-bat, and it was him doing what he did and that was leading the way. He was definitely a leader as a player—big time. He was all about winning, and he wanted everyone else to be about winning, too.

It was such a great home run because of the drama attached to it: the injuries, not knowing whether he could even stand up, and our scout guaranteeing that Eckersley would throw a back-door slider. And, there was Lasorda's emotional decision [to bat Gibson]—genius. So many things came into play, and it was very magical. —Ricky Horton, 61, St. Louis Cardinals announcer.

Since Orel Hershiser struck out Tony Phillips to end the 1988 World Series, more than a generation has passed—33 years, to be exact. In all that time the Dodgers have won only a single World Series, sad irony for a team that won four championships in ten years during the 1950s and 1960s and was long considered the National League's most admired franchise. During the same 33-year period the A's also won only one World Series: in 1989, with many of the same players who lost to the Dodgers the previous season contributing. The A's organization [including the Kansas City A's] also leads the Dodgers in total championships won with nine compared with the Dodgers' seven. The storied Dodgers, it seems, may arguably be less storied than the Oakland A's.

To emphasize the team's lament, a Chicagoan suggested that after the Cubs won the 2016 World Series to end their 108-year drought, the Windy City team had won more world championships than the Dodgers had over the previous quarter-century. While true at the time, that's no longer the case.

Like the Dodgers franchise, many of the players, broadcasters, and others involved in the 1988 World Series have also disappeared from the spotlight. After his Game One home run planted an exclamation mark on both the 1988 season and the highly favored Oakland A's, **Kirk Gibson** was named National League MVP, receiving an award he later auctioned off for $110,000, with the proceeds going to support his private foundation. It marked a high point of his career, although that peak quickly rolled into a valley. Gibson never again experienced such remarkable success, and his career slowly began to taper off. He never again came to bat as many times as he did that season, nor did he ever again record as many hits, doubles, home runs, or RBI. His batting average never again approached the .290 that he charted during that MVP season,

Still, the Dodges stuck with their World Series hero for two more seasons, both of them sub-par ones. In 1989, his 11th season in the major leagues, Gibson batted just 253 times and produced 54 hits, nine home runs, and 28 RBI; his batting average was a less-than-modest .213. In 1990, his last season with the Dodgers, he batted 315 times and recorded 82 hits with eight home runs and 38 RBI. His batting average was a respectable .260.

Gibson signed as a free agent with the Kansas City Royals in 1991 and his numbers improved, as he hit 16 home runs and drove in 55 runs. He was traded to Pittsburgh the next year, was released, briefly retired, then returned to Detroit in 1993 where he finished out his career in 1995—16 years after it began in the Motor City. During his final major-league season Gibson hit nine home runs and drove in 55 runs, batting a workmanlike .260. Then it was over.

After retiring as a player, Gibson managed an investment company for a short period, then worked as a color analyst for Fox Sports Net Detroit covering Detroit Tigers games; he also co-hosted a sports talk program. Eventually, Gibson heard the call of baseball again and he joined the Tigers as a coach, remaining in that position from 2003 through 2005. He later became a bench coach with the Arizona Diamondbacks and was named manager in 2010, a position he held through the 2014 season. The high point of that transition occurred when Gibson was named National League Manager of the Year in 2011 after his team won its first National League West Division title in franchise history. Three years later his fortunes changed and he was fired after his team posted a forgettable 63-96 record.

Gibson's personal life came into sharp focus in 2015 when he revealed that he had been diagnosed with Parkinson's disease; as a result, he established the Kirk Gibson Foundation supporting Parkinson's research. While the disease has affected him physically, it hasn't stopped him from appearing in public. On March 29, 2018, Gibson threw out the first pitch to open the Dodgers' 2018 season, following that up by receiving a first pitch in the 2018 World Series thrown by, who else, Eckersley. That same year, the team dedicated the "Kirk Gibson 88 Seat" in right field, the locus where his miraculous home run likely fell to earth. The seat, appropriately painted blue, bears Gibson's permanent autograph. Curiously, Gibson confided to teammates during a 30-year reunion of the 1988 World Series victory that he feels increasingly uncomfortable discussing his Game One home run, believing any of his teammates could have had the same good fortune. Still, the Kirk Gibson 88 Seat belongs to only one man: Gibson.

"No one recognized the importance or the opportunity of the moment more than Kirk," Claire said. "He, perhaps more than anybody in the ballpark, had the vision of what could happen." He added, "That was the game and that was the Series."

Unlike Gibson, **Dennis Eckersley** was at the zenith of his prowess as a major league ballplayer when the 1988 World Series came to a disastrous close for him and his A's. Already 34 years of age when he walked away from the pitching mound after surrendering the game-winning home run to Gibson, Eckersley would pitch for another decade, averaging 32 saves per season during that period of time. More immediately, over the two years that followed the 1988 Series, Eckersley would lower his ERA by nearly a run each season, to 1.56 in 1989 and 0.61 in 1990, cementing his legacy as one of the great relief pitchers ever.

The A's returned to the World Series in 1989, with Eckersley pitching only 1.2 innings and earning a save, and again in 1990, when he lost a game, recorded zero saves, and posted an ERA of 6.75. His best season as a professional may have been 1992 when he saved a whopping 51 games on the strength of a sterling 1.91 ERA and was voted the American League's Most Valuable Player. His record that season, his sixth and final one as an all-star, was 7-1. In 1997, his 23rd year in the major leagues, the 43-year-oldl Eckersley was still effective, saving 36 games.

After retiring in 1998, Eckersley worked as a studio analyst covering the Boston Red Sox. In 2005 his number 43 was retired by the Oakland A's; the following year his high school renamed its baseball field Dennis Eckersley Field. Eckersley had come full circle.

Dennis Eckersley (National Baseball Hall of Fame).

Two decades after retiring from baseball, Eckersley still ranks seventh on the list of all-time major-league save leaders. He remains one of the most effective relief pitchers in the history of the game—October 15, 1988, notwithstanding.

"I was supposed to be there," Eckersley, seemingly resigned to his place in history, told a reporter 30 years later. "I was supposed to be a part of it, and I can accept that."[1]

While immensely successful as an on-field manager, **Tom Lasorda's** life off the field was not without its challenges. Three years after beating Oakland in the 1988 World Series, Lasorda's son, Tom Lasorda Jr., known affectionately as Spunky, died of pneumonia. Five years after that, Lasorda suffered a serious health crisis of his own, a heart attack that forced him to retire from the game he loved rather than endure the daily rigors that a major-league manager must face; he maintained an office at Dodger Stadium until his death in 2021 and was long considered a beloved member of the Dodgers family. Despite his retirement, Lasorda guided the U.S. Olympic baseball team to a gold medal in the 2000 Olympic Games, with the U.S. shutting out Cuba 4-0 in the final game. Although he suffered another heart attack in 2012, Lasorda continued to work and travel and remained a foremost ambassador for the game of baseball. Over 19 full seasons as manager of the Dodgers—he was 2-2 his partial first season and his final one was cut short because of poor health—Lasorda averaged 82 wins per year. His 1988 matchup against the Oakland A's marked his final and perhaps most satisfying World Series appearance.

"We beat 'em," Lasorda said shortly before his death. "I told our guys we were gonna beat 'em."

In beating the A's, Lasorda brought one baseball truth into focus: "The game's never over until nine innings are completed."

With the World Series loss in 1988, manager **Tony La Russa** was even more motivated the next season, and his team won the world championship. Players attributed their victory in the 1989 Series to the tough loss the Dodgers inflicted on them in 1988. "The fact that we lost the World Series in '88 was a huge factor in winning it the next year," the third baseman Lansford said. "We felt we didn't finish it off that season. We were more determined the next season to finish what we didn't do in 1988."

After performing as a player for five seasons and achieving a modest .199 lifetime batting average, Tony La Russa left his mark as a field manager. He managed in the major leagues from 1979 to 2011, a total of 33-three seasons, winning six pennants and three World Series—one

Series with Oakland and two with St. Louis. His 2,728 managerial wins with the Chicago White Sox, Oakland A's, and St. Louis Cardinals ranks third on the all-time list behind the great Connie Mack and John McGraw.

La Russa was the first manager to win all-star games in both leagues and the second to win a World Series in both circuits; he won his first World Series with Oakland in 1989. Named American League Manager of the Year three times and National League Manager of the Year once, La Russa was inducted into the Hall of Fame in 2014.

After retiring in 2011, La Russa was involved with various philanthropic activities. He also worked as a special assistant to the commissioner of baseball and served on a committee that established a replay system that owners approved in 2014. His number 10 was retired by the Cardinals in 2012. In 2014 the Arizona Diamondbacks—managed that season, ironically, by Kirk Gibson—named him the team's chief baseball officer, and in 2020 he signed to manage the Chicago White Sox, a position he still holds. More than 30 years after the fact, La Russa still has difficulty watching replays of Gibson's home run.

After 1988, **Vin Scully** broadcast Dodger games for another 28 seasons, and his call of Gibson's monumental home run may have been his greatest—certainly the greatest in the latter half of his long career. Like Lasorda, Scully's personal life also was fraught with difficulty: in 1972 his wife, Joan, died in her sleep of an accidental medication overdose after 14 years of marriage. Twenty-two years later, in 1994, his 33-year-old son, Michael, died in a helicopter crash. Finally, in 2021 his second wife Sandra died of complications from ALS—Lou Gehrig's Disease. Through most of it, Scully remained a fixture behind the Dodger microphone. Dating back to his Brooklyn Dodger days, the venerable announcer called 13 World Series for the organization, six of which the team won. Scully, who retired in 2016, received the Ford C. Frick Award for broadcast excellence from the Baseball Hall of Fame in 1982 and was the recipient of a Lifetime Achievement Emmy Award in 1995. He concedes, perhaps facetiously, that his greatest achievement for the Dodgers may have been

Vin Scully in 2004 (courtesy of the University of Southern California).

getting Gibson off the trainer's table to hit in Game One of the 1988 World Series.

Did Scully set in motion events that resulted in the greatest home run ever? "There couldn't have been any better," Lasorda said of the blast.

After the 1988 season concluded, **Jose Canseco** continued to excel as a player, leading the American League in home runs with 44 in 1991. He retired in 2001 with numerous awards and honors to his credit. In addition to the MVP award he earned in 1988, Canseco had been Rookie of the Year in 1986, was a six-time all-star, and won four Silver Slugger Awards as the best offensive player at his position. Canseco earned some non-baseball notoriety in 2014 when he accidentally shot his finger off while cleaning a gun, making him the poster boy for athletically inspired, weapons-related, finger-detaching gun accidents. That incident aside, the 1988 World Series remains a black mark on an otherwise spotless baseball record: the grand slam in Game One was his only hit in 19 at-bats.

Mark McGwire improved steadily following the 1988 World Series, slugging 42 home runs in 1992, 52 in 1996, 58 in 1997, 70 in 1998, and 65 in 1999. During his 16-year career he led the American League in home runs four times, RBI once, and various other less conspicuous offensive categories numerous times.

Like Canseco, McGwire also had a dismal 1988 World Series, going 1 for 17 over the five games against Los Angeles. Again like Canseco, his only hit was a home run. Combined, the two sluggers were 2 for 36 in the World Series. Ironically, from 2013 to 2015 McGwire proudly wore blue and white as the Dodgers' hitting coach.

After pitching two near-perfect innings as the setup man for Alejandro Pena in Game One, **Brian Holton** was on top of the world. It didn't last. Despite achieving an ERA of 1.70 over 84 innings pitched that season, which ended with a personal-best 17-2/3-inning scoreless streak, Holton would never throw another pitch for the Dodgers, who traded him to Baltimore after the World Series; his World Series ring arrived in the mail. Two years later, Holton was out of baseball, a forgotten man from a team that everyone remembered.[2]

Mitch Poole joined the Dodgers as a ballboy in 1985 and was working as a batboy when Gibson hit his historic home run. Fittingly, the following

Mark McGwire at USC (courtesy of the University of Southern California).

season he was promoted to assistant clubhouse manager, and today, 36 years later, Poole is a fixture with the club, working as the team's visiting clubhouse manager. By virtue of his Corinthian baseball spirit and the assistance he rendered to Gibson during Game One of the 1988 World Series, Poole, like Gibson, remains an important footnote in Dodgers history.

"I'll always be . . . linked to Kirk Gibson," Poole said. 'I have no choice, [I'm] linked to him forever."[3]

Rick Dempsey, who went 1 for 5 with a double and an RBI in his final World Series, retired in 1992, ending a career that had begun in 1969. He remembers the 1988 Series with a sense of irony.

"On paper, we were the worst World Series team ever," he said. "[Gibson] just turned it around. It had to be the greatest moment in World Series history."

APPENDIX[1]

WORLD SERIES ROSTER [DODGERS]

Dave Anderson	Tim Belcher
Mike Davis	Rick Dempsey
Kirk Gibson	Jose Gonzales
Alfredo Griffin	Jeff Hamilton
Mickey Hatcher	Danny Heep
Orel Hershiser	Brian Holton
Jay Howell	Tim Leary
Mike Marshall	Alejandro Pena
Steve Sax	Mike Scioscia
John Shelby	Franklin Stubbs
John Tudor	Tracy Woodson

WORLD SERIES ROSTER [A'S]

Don Baylor	Todd Burns
Greg Cadaret	Jose Canseco
Storm Davis	Dennis Eckersley
Mike Gallego	Ron Hassey
Dave Henderson	Rick Honeycutt
Glenn Hubbard	Stan Javier
Carney Lansford	Mark McGwire
Gene Nelson	Dave Parker
Tony Phillips	Eric Plunk
Luis Polonia	Terry Steinbach
Dave Stewart	Walt Weiss
Bob Welch	Curt Young

GAME ONE STARTING LINEUP, A'S

Carney Lansford 3B
Jose Canseco RF
Mark McGwire 1B
Glenn Hubbard 2B
Dave Stewart P

Dave Henderson CF
Dave Parker LF
Terry Steinbach C
Walt Weiss SS

GAME ONE STARTING LINEUP, DODGERS

Steve Sax 2B
Mickey Hatcher LF
John Shelby CF
Jeff Hamilton 3B
Tim Belcher P

Franklin Stubbs 1B
Mike Marshall RF
Mike Scioscia C
Alfredo Griffin SS

GAME ONE, BOX SCORE[2]

BATTING

OAKLAND A's	AB	R	H	RBI	BB	SO
Lansford 3b	4	1	0	0	1	1
Henderson cf	5	0	2	0	0	2
Canseco rf	4	1	1	4	0	1
Parker lf	2	0	0	0	2	0
Javier pr, lf	1	0	1	0	0	0
McGwire 1b	3	0	0	0	2	0
Steinbach c	4	0	1	0	0	1
Hassey c	0	0	0	0	0	0
Hubbard 2b	4	1	2	0	0	0
Weiss ss	4	0	0	0	0	1
Stewart p	3	1	0	0	1	3
Eckersley p	0	0	0	0	0	0
Totals	34	4	7	4	6	9

2B: Henderson; HR: Canseco

L.A. DODGERS	AB	R	H	RBI	BB	SO
Sax 2b	3	1	1	0	0	0
Stubbs 1b	4	0	0	0	0	0
Hatcher lf	3	1	1	2	1	1
Marshall rf	4	1	1	0	0	1
Shelby cf	4	0	1	0	0	1
Scioscia c	4	0	1	1	0	0
Hamilton 3b	4	0	0	0	0	2
Griffin ss	2	0	1	0	1	0
Davis ph	0	1	0	0	1	0
Belcher p	0	0	0	0	0	0
Heep ph	1	0	0	0	0	0
Leary p	0	0	0	0	0	0
Woodson ph	1	0	0	0	0	0
Holton p	0	0	0	0	0	0
Gonzalez ph	1	0	0	0	0	1
Pena p	0	0	0	0	0	0
Gibson p	1	1	1	2	0	0
Totals	32	5	7	5	3	6

HR: Hatcher; Gibson

PITCHING

OAKLAND A's	IP	H	R	ER	BB	SO
Stewart	8	6	3	3	2	5
Eckersley L[0-1]	0.2	1	2	2	1	1
Totals	8.2	7	5	5	3	6

L.A. DODGERS	IP	H	R	ER	BB	SO
Belcher	2	3	4	4	4	3
Leary	3	3	0	0	1	3
Holton	2	0	0	0	1	0
Pena W[1-0]	2	1	0	0	0	3
Totals	9	7	4	4	6	9

2018 WORLD SERIES BATTING STATS
[Listed by player batting average][3]

LOS ANGELES DODGERS

NAME	G	AB	R	H	2B	3B	HR	RBI	BB	SO	BA
Kirk Gibson	1	1	1	1	0	0	1	2	0	0	1.000
Orel Hershiser	2	3	1	3	2	0	0	1	0	0	1.000
Mickey Hatcher	5	19	5	7	1	0	2	5	1	3	.368
Steve Sax	5	20	3	6	0	0	0	0	1	1	.300
Franklin Stubbs	5	17	3	5	2	0	0	2	1	3	.294
Danny Heep	3	8	0	2	1	0	0	0	0	2	.250
Mike Marshall	5	13	2	3	0	1	1	3	0	5	.231
John Shelby	5	18	0	4	1	0	0	1	2	7	.222
Mike Scioscia	4	14	0	3	0	0	0	1	0	2	.214
Rick Dempsey	2	5	0	1	1	0	0	1	1	2	.200
Alfredo Griffin	5	16	2	3	0	0	0	0	2	4	.188
Mike Davis	4	7	4	1	0	0	1	2	4	0	.143
Jeff Hamilton	5	19	1	2	0	0	0	0	1	4	.105
Jose Gonzalez	4	2	0	0	0	0	0	0	0	2	.000
Dave Anderson	1	1	0	0	0	0	0	0	0	1	.000
Tim Belcher	2	0	0	0	0	0	0	0	0	0	–
Brian Holton	1	0	0	0	0	0	0	0	0	0	–
Jay Howell	2	0	0	0	0	0	0	0	0	0	–
Tim Leary	2	0	0	0	0	0	0	0	0	0	–
Alejandro Pena	2	0	0	0	0	0	0	0	0	0	–
John Tudor	1	0	0	0	0	0	0	0	0	0	–
Tracy Woodson	4	4	0	0	0	0	0	1	0	0	–
Totals	70	167	21	41	8	1	5	19	13	36	.246

OAKLAND ATHLETICS

NAME	G	AB	R	H	2B	3B	HR	RBI	BB	SO	BA
Stan Javier	3	4	0	2	0	0	0	2	0	1	.500
Terry Steinbach	3	11	0	4	1	0	0	0	0	2	.364
Dave Henderson	5	20	1	6	2	0	0	1	2	7	.300
Ron Hassey	5	8	0	2	0	0	0	1	3	3	.250
Glenn Hubbard	4	12	2	3	0	0	0	0	1	0	.250
Tony Phillips	2	4	1	1	0	0	0	0	1	2	.250
Dave Parker	4	15	0	3	0	0	0	0	2	4	.200
Carney Lansford	5	18	2	3	0	0	0	1	2	2	.167
Luis Polonia	3	9	1	1	0	0	0	0	0	2	.111
Walt Weiss	5	16	1	1	0	0	0	0	0	2	.063
Mark McGwire	5	17	1	1	0	0	1	1	3	4	.059
Jose Canseco	5	19	1	1	0	0	1	5	2	5	.053
Don Baylor	1	1	0	0	0	0	0	0	0	1	.000
Dave Stewart	2	3	1	0	0	0	0	0	1	3	.000
Storm Davis	2	1	0	0	0	0	0	0	0	1	.000
Todd Burns	1	0	0	0	0	0	0	0	0	0	–
Greg Cadaret	3	0	0	0	0	0	0	0	0	0	–
Dennis Eckersley	2	0	0	0	0	0	0	0	0	0	–
Mike Gallego	1	0	0	0	0	0	0	0	0	0	–
Rick Honeycutt	3	0	0	0	0	0	0	0	0	0	–
Gene Nelson	3	0	0	0	0	0	0	0	0	0	–
Eric Plunk	2	0	0	0	0	0	0	0	0	0	–
Bob Welch	1	0	0	0	0	0	0	0	0	0	–
Curt Young	1	0	0	0	0	0	0	0	0	0	–
Totals	71	158	11	28	3	0	2	11	17	41	.177

WORLD SERIES PITCHING STATS
[Descending by player ERA][4]

LOS ANGELES DODGERS

NAME	G	GS	ERA	W	L	SV	CG	IP	H	R	ER	BB	SO
John Tudor	1	1	0.00	0	0	0	0	1.1	0	0	0	0	1
Brian Holton	1	0	0.00	0	0	0	0	2.0	0	0	0	1	0
Al. Pena	2	0	0.00	1	0	0	0	0.1	0	0	0	0	0
Orel Hershiser	2	2	1.00	2	0	0	2	18.0	7	2	2	6	17
Tim Leary	2	0	1.35	0	0	0	0	6.2	6	1	1	1	4
Jay Howell	2	0	3.38	0	1	1	1	2.2	3	1	1	1	2
Tim Belcher	2	2	6.23	1	0	0	0	8.2	10	7	6	6	10
Totals	12	5	2.03	4	1	1	2	44.1	28	11	10	17	41

OAKLAND ATHLETICS

NAME	G	GS	ERA	W	L	SV	CG	IP	H	R	ER	BB	SO
Todd Burns	1	0	0.00	0	0	0	0	0.1	0	0	0	0	0
Greg Cadaret	3	0	0.00	0	0	0	0	2.0	2	2	2	2	3
Eric Plunk	2	0	0.00	0	0	0	0	1.2	0	0	0	0	3
Curt Young	1	0	0.00	0	0	0	0	1.0	1	0	0	0	0
Rick Honeycutt	3	0	0.00	1	0	0	0	3.1	0	0	0	0	5
Gene Nelson	3	0	1.42	0	0	0	0	6.1	4	1	1	3	3
Bob Welch	1	1	1.80	0	0	0	0	5.0	6	1	1	3	8
Dave Stewart	2	2	3.14	0	1	0	0	14.1	12	7	5	5	5
D. Eckersley	2	0	10.80	0	1	0	0	1.2	2	2	2	1	2
Storm Davis	2	2	11.25	0	2	0	0	8.0	14	10	10	1	7
Totals	20	5	3.92	1	4	0	0	43.2	41	21	19	13	36

GAME ONE, PLAY BY PLAY[5]

A's 1ST: Lansford called out on strikes; Henderson singles to center; Canseco hit by pitch [Henderson to second]; Parker flies to center; McGwire walks [Henderson to third, Canseco to second]; Steinbach flies to center; 0 R, 1 H, 0 E, 3 LOB. Athletics 0, Dodgers 0.

DODGERS 1ST: Sax hit by a pitch; both teams warned by HP umpire Doug Harvey; Stubbs flies to center; Stewart balks [Sax to second]; Hatcher homers [Sax scores]; Marshall strikes out; Shelby grounds out [first unassisted]; 2 R, 1 H, 0 E, 0 LOB. Athletics 0, Dodgers 2.

A's 2ND: Hubbard singles to left; Weiss was called out on strikes; Stewart walks [Hubbard to second]; Lansford walks [Hubbard to third, Stewart to second]; Henderson strikes out; Canseco homers [Hubbard, Stewart, Lansford score]; Parker walks; McGwire forces Parker [shortstop to second]; 4 R, 2 H, 0 E, 1 LOB. Athletics 4, Dodgers 2.

DODGERS 2ND: Scioscia pops to shortstop; Hamilton grounds out [shortstop to first]; Griffin singles to right; Heep bats for Belcher; Heep grounds out [shortstop to first]; 0 R, 1 H, 0 E, 1 LOB. Athletics 4, Dodgers 2.

A's 3RD: Leary replaces Heep [pitching]; Steinbach singles to third; Hubbard singles to left [Steinbach to second]; Weiss flies to left; Stewart strikes out; Lansford forces Hubbard [shortstop unassisted]; 0 R, 2 H, 0 E, 2 LOB. Athletics 4, Dodgers 2.

DODGERS 3RD: Sax flies to right; Stubbs flies to left; Hatcher walks; Marshall lines to third; 0 R, 0 H, 0 E, 1 LOB. Athletics 4, Dodgers 2.

A's 4TH: Henderson doubles; Canseco reaches on a fielder's choice [Henderson out at third, shortstop to third]; Parker grounds out [pitcher to first, Canseco staying at first]; Dave Parker called for interference for running in fair territory; Canseco steals second; McGwire walks intentionally; Steinbach strikes out; 0 R, 1 H, 0 E, 2 LOB. Athletics 4, Dodgers 2.

DODGERS 4TH: Shelby strikes out; Scioscia flies to center; Hamilton strikes out; 0 R, 0 H, 0 E, 0 LOB. Athletics 4, Dodgers 2.

A's 5TH: Hubbard grounds out [shortstop to first]; Weiss grounds out [first unassisted]; Stewart called out on strikes; 0 R, 0 H, 0 E, 0 LOB. Athletics 4, Dodgers 2.

DODGERS 5TH: Griffin walks; Woodson bats for Leary; Woodson forces Griffin [shortstop to second, Woodson to first]; Sax flies to center; Stewart throws a wild pitch [Woodson to second]; Stubbs grounds out [first unassisted]; 0 R, 0 H, 0 E, 1 LOB. Athletics 4, Dodgers 2.

A's 6TH: Holton replaces Woodson [pitching]; Lansford lines to center; Henderson grounds out [shortstop to first]; Canseco grounds out [third to first]; 0 R, 0 H, 0 E, 0 LOB. Athletics 4, Dodgers 2.

DODGERS 6TH: Hatcher lines to center; Marshall singles to right; Shelby singles to center [Marshall to second]; Scioscia singles to left [Marshall scores, Shelby to second]; Hamilton grounds into a double play [third to first, Shelby out at third]; 1 R, 3 H, 0 E, 1 LOB. Athletics 4, Dodgers 3.

A's 7TH: Parker walks; Javier runs for Parker; McGwire grounds out [pitcher to first, Javier to second]; Steinbach lines to third; Hubbard pops to right; 0 R, 0 H, 0 E, 1 LOB. Athletics 4, Dodgers 3.

DODGERS 7TH: Javier stays in game [playing LF]; On a bunt, Griffin grounds out [third to first]; Gonzales bats for Holton; Gonzalez strikes out; Sax singles to left; Sax steals second; Stubbs flies to right; 0 R, 1 H, 0 E, 1 LOB. Athletics 4, Dodgers 3.

A's 8TH: Pena replaces Gonzales [pitching]; Weiss pops to second; Stewart called out on strikes; Lansford grounds out [second to first]; 0 R, 0 H, 0 E, 0 LOB. Athletics 4, Dodgers 3.

DODGERS 8TH: Hatcher called out on strikes; Marshall pops to second; Shelby flies out to right; 0 R, 0 H, 0 E, 0 LOB. Athletics 4, Dodgers 3.

A's 9TH: Henderson strikes out; Canseco strikes out; Javier singles to shortstop; McGwire flies to right; 0 R, 1 H, 0 E, 1 LOB. Athletics 4, Dodgers 3.

DODGERS 9TH: Hassey replaces Steinbach [playing C]; Eckersley replaces Stewart [pitching]; Scioscia popped to shortstop; Hamilton called out on strikes; Davis bats for Griffin; Davis walks; Gibson bats for Pena; Davis steals second; Gibson homers [Davis scores]; 2 R, 1 H, 0 E, 0 LOB. Athletics 4, Dodgers 5.

FINAL TOTALS	R	H	E	LOB
A's	4	7	0	10
Dodgers	5	7	0	5

KIRK GIBSON'S MAJOR-LEAGUE STATISTICS[6]

YR	TEAM	LEAGUE	AB	H	2B	3B	HR	BI	AVG
1979	DET	AL	38	9	3	0	1	4	.237
1980	DET	AL	175	46	2	1	9	16	.263
1981	DET	AL	290	95	11	3	9	40	.328
1982	DET	AL	266	74	16	2	8	35	.278
1983	DET	AL	401	91	12	9	15	51	.227
1984	DET	AL	531	150	23	10	27	91	.282
1985	DET	AL	581	167	37	5	29	97	.287
1986	DET	AL	441	118	11	2	28	86	.268
1987	DET	AL	487	135	25	3	24	79	.277
1988	LA	NL	542	157	28	1	25	76	.290
1989	LA	NL	253	54	8	2	9	28	.213
1990	LA	NL	315	82	20	0	8	38	.260
1991	KC	AL	462	109	17	6	16	55	.236
1992	PIT	NL	56	11	0	0	2	5	.196
1993	DET	AL	403	105	18	6	13	62	.261
1994	DET	AL	330	91	17	2	23	72	.276
1995	DET	AL	227	59	12	2	9	35	.260
Totals:									
17	4	AL/NL	5798	1553	260	54	255	870	.268

DENNIS ECKERSLEY'S MAJOR-LEAGUE STATISTICS[7]

YR	TEAM	LEAGUE	W	L	G	GS	CG	SV	SO	IP	ERA
1975	CLE	AL	13	7	34	24	6	2	152	186.2	2.60
1976	CLE	AL	13	12	36	30	9	1	200	199.1	3.43
1977	CLE	AL	14	13	33	33	12	0	191	247.1	3.53
1978	BOS	AL	20	8	35	35	16	0	162	268.1	2.99
1979	BOS	AL	17	10	33	33	17	0	150	246.2	2.99
1980	BOS	AL	12	14	30	30	8	0	121	197.2	4.28
1981	BOS	AL	9	8	23	23	8	0	79	154.0	4.27
1982	BOS	AL	13	13	33	33	11	0	127	224.1	3.73
1983	BOS	AL	9	13	28	28	2	0	77	176.1	5.61
1984	BOS	AL	4	4	9	9	2	0	33	64.2	5.01
1984	CHI	NL	10	8	24	24	2	0	81	160.1	3.03
1985	CHI	NL	11	7	25	25	6	0	117	169.1	3.08
1986	CHI	NL	6	11	33	32	1	0	137	201.0	4.57
1987	OAK	AL	6	8	54	2	0	16	113	115.2	3.03
1988	OAK	AL	4	2	60	0	0	45	70	72.2	2.35
1989	OAK	AL	4	0	51	0	0	33	55	57.2	1.56
1990	OAK	AL	4	2	63	0	0	48	73	73.1	0.61
1991	OAK	AL	5	4	67	0	0	43	87	76.0	2.96
1992	OAK	AL	7	1	69	0	0	51	93	80.0	1.91
1993	OAK	AL	2	4	64	0	0	36	80	67.0	4.16
1994	OAK	AL	5	4	45	0	0	19	47	44.1	4.26
1995	OAK	AL	4	6	52	0	0	29	40	50.1	4.83
1996	STL	NL	0	6	63	0	0	30	49	60.0	3.30
1997	STL	NL	1	5	57	0	0	36	45	53.0	3.91
1998	BOS	AL	4	1	50	0	0	1	22	39.2	4.76
Totals:											
24	5	AL/NL	197	171	1071	361	100	390	2401	3285.2	3.50

KIRK GIBSON'S WORLD SERIES STATISTICS[8]

YR	TEAM	LEAGUE	AB	H	2B	3B	HR	BI	AVG
2	2	AL/NL	19	7	0	0	3	9	.368

DENNIS ECKERSLEY'S WORLD SERIES STATISTICS[9]

YR	TEAM	LEAGUE	W	L	SV	IP	SO	HR	ERA
3	1	AL	0	2	1	4.2	3	1	5.79

WORLD SERIES WALK-OFF HOME RUNS[10]

1. 1949, Tommy Henrich, New York Yankees versus Brooklyn Dodgers, Game One: Henrich broke a scoreless tie in the bottom of the ninth inning by homering off Brooklyn's Don Newcombe to win the game, 1-0. The Yankees won the Series, 4-1.

2. 1954, Dusty Rhodes, New York Giants versus Cleveland Indians, Game One: In the bottom of the 10th inning, New York's Rhodes broke a 2-2 tie with a three-run, pinch-hit home run off Bob Lemon to win the game, 5-2. The Giants swept Cleveland, 4-0.

3. 1957, Eddie Matthews, Milwaukee Braves versus New York Yankees, Game Four: With the score tied 5-5 in the 10th inning, Matthews homered off Yankee Bob Grim to win the game, 7-5. The Braves won the series, 4-3.

4. 1960, Bill Mazeroski, Pittsburgh Pirates versus New York Yankees, Game Seven: The score was tied 9-9 in the ninth inning when Mazeroski homered off the Yankees' Ralph Terry to win the game, 10-9. The Pirates won the Series, 4-3.

5. 1964, Mickey Mantle, New York Yankees versus St. Louis Cardinals, Game Three: Mantle broke a 1-1 tie by homering off the Cardinals'

Barney Schultz in the ninth inning to win the game, 2-1. The Cardinals won the Series, 4-3.

6. 1975, Carlton Fisk, Boston Red Sox versus Cincinnati Reds, Game Six: In the bottom of the 12th inning, with the score tied 6-6, Fisk homered off Cincinnati's Pat Darcy to win the game for Boston, 7-6. The Reds won the Series, 4-3.

7. **1988, Kirk Gibson, Los Angeles Dodgers versus Oakland Athletics, Game One: With the Dodgers trailing, 4-3, the pinch hitter Gibson homered off Oakland's Dennis Eckersley to win the game, 5-4. The homer is one of two that have won World Series games for a team that was losing at the time the blast was hit. The Dodgers won the Series, 4-1.**

8. 1988, Mark McGwire, Oakland A's versus Los Angeles Dodgers, Game Three: McGwire homered off Dodgers' closer Jay Howell to break a 1-1 tie in the ninth inning and win the game, 2-1. Of the 15 walk-off home runs in World Series history, two occurred during this series. The Dodgers won the Series, 4-1.

9. 1991, Kirby Puckett, Minnesota Twins versus Atlanta Braves, Game Six: The score was tied 3-3 in the 11th inning when Puckett homered off the Braves' Charlie Leibrandt to win the game, 4-3. Minnesota won the Series, 4-3.

10. 1993, Joe Carter, Toronto Blue Jays versus Philadelphia Phillies, Game Six: With his team trailing 6-5 in the ninth inning, Carter homered off Phillies closer Mitch Williams to win the game, 8-6. Toronto won the Series, 4-2, and Carter's homer marked only the second time—Gibson's was the other—that a walk-off home run had brought his team from behind to win a World Series game.

11. 1999, Chad Curtis, New York Yankees versus Atlanta Braves, Game Three: With the score tied 5-5 in the 10th inning, Chad Curtis swatted a pitch from Braves' pitcher Mike Remlinger to win the game in

the bottom of the ninth inning, 6-5. The Yankees would sweep the Series, 4-0.

12. 2001, Derek Jeter, New York Yankees versus Arizona Diamondbacks, Game Four: With the score tied 3-3 in the 10th inning, Jeter homered off Byung-hyun Kim to win the game, 4-3. The Diamondbacks won the series, 4-3.

13. 2003, Alex Gonzales, Florida Marlins versus New York Yankees, Game Four: Florida won the game, 4-3, on a 12th-inning, tie-breaking home run by Gonzales off Yankees' pitcher Jeff Weaver. Florida won the Series, 4-2.

14. 2005, Scott Podsednik, Chicago White Sox versus Houston Astros, Game Two: The score was tied 6-6 in the ninth inning when Podsednik homered off Astros pitcher Brad Lidge to give his team a 7-6 win. The White Sox won the Series, 4-0.

15. 2011, David Freese, St. Louis Cardinals versus Texas Rangers, Game Six: The score was tied 9-9 in the 11th inning when Freese came to bat, homering off the Rangers' Mark Lowe to win the game, 10-9. The Cardinals won the Series, 4-3.

NOTES

PROLOGUE
1. "1988 World Series, Game One: A's @ Dodgers," youtube.com, https://www.youtube.com/watch?v=b1_0373UNDc [13 June 2018].
2. "Opening Day: April 10, 1962," walteromalley.com, https://www.walteromalley.com/en/dodger-stadium/opening-day/Introduction [2 June 2018].
3. "Bobby Thomson, former N.J. resident known for 'Shot Heard 'Round the World' home run, dies at 86." New Jersey Star-Ledger, Aug. 17, 2010.
4. Alby Oxenreiter, "Pirates's Bill Mazeroski Reflects on Iconic World Series Home Run," wxpi.com, https://www.wpxi.com/news/proud-to-be-from-pittsburgh/pirates-bill-mazeroski-reflects-on-iconic-world-series-home-run/622724925 [30 May 2018].
5. "Opening Day: April 10, 1962," walteromalley.com, https://www.walteromalley.com/en/dodger-stadium/opening-day/Introduction [2 June 2018].

CHAPTER 1: GAME ONE
1. "Debbie Gibson Performs National Anthem," youtube.com, https://www.youtube.com/watch?v=75oe33I8sAE [1 June 2018].
2. "Hershiser Hurls Dodgers to 6-0 Flag Clincher," *Los Angeles Times*, 13 October 1988, 1.
3. Scott Ostler, "Hatcher, the Unsung Hero, Leaves Mets Singing the Blues," *Los Angeles Times*, 13 October 1988, 48.
4. "1988 World Series, Game One: A's at Dodgers," youtube.com, https://www.youtube.com/watch?v=b1_0373UNDc [1 June 2018].
5. "Opening Day: April 10, 1962," walteromalley.com, https://www.walteromalley.com/en/dodger-stadium/opening-day/Introduction [6 June 2018].
6. "1988 World Series Game One, Athletics at Dodgers, October 15," baseball-reference.com, https://www.baseball-reference.com/boxes/LAN/LAN198810150.shtml [5 June 2018].
7. Ibid.

CHAPTER 2: THE ROOKIE
1. Eric Stephen, "1988 Dodgers player profile: Tim Belcher, the rookie," truebluela.com, https://www.truebluela.com/2013/1/2/3546446/tim-belcher-1988-dodgers [9 June 2018].

CHAPTER 4: FIRST BLOOD — 2-0

1. Jacob Unruh, "Collected Wisdom of former Sooner, Dodger Mickey Hatcher," newsok.com, https://newsok.com/article/5591027/collected-wisdom-of-former-sooner-dodger-mickey-hatcher [13 June 2018].
2. Ibid.
3. Craig Minami, "1988 Dodgers player profile: Mickey Hatcher, more than a stunt man," truebluela.com, https://www.truebluela.com/2013/1/9/3826798/mickey-hatcher-1988-dodgers [13 June 2018].
4. Ibid.
5. Ibid.
6. "Mike Schmidt." Baseball.org. http://baseballhall.org/hof/schmidt-mike [accessed March 14, 2017].
7. Scott Ostler, "Hatcher, the Unsung Hero, Leaves Mets Singing the Blues," *Los Angeles Times*, 13 October 1988, 48.

CHAPTER 5: SLAM — 4-2

1. "1988 World Series, Game 1: A's @ Dodgers," youtube.com, https://www.youtube.com/watch?v=b1_0373UNDc [21 June 2018].
2. Michael Martinez, "Athletics's Pitchers are Forming a Batting Rotation," nytimes.com, https://www.nytimes.com/1988/10/12/sports/athletics-pitchers-are-forming-a-batting-rotation.html [21 June 2018].
3. "1988 World Series, Game 1: A's @ Dodgers," youtube.com, https://www.youtube.com/watch?v=b1_0373UNDc [22 June 2018].
4. "World Series Grand Slams," espn.com [Associated Press], http://www.espn.com/espn/wire/_/section/mlb/id/3654103 [25 June 2018].
5. Joseph Wancho, "October 10, 1920: A game of World Series firsts: unassisted triple play and grand slam," sabr.org, https://sabr.org/gamesproj/game/october-10-1920-world-series-game-firsts-unassisted-triple-play-and-grand-slam [26 June 2018].
6. "Career Leaders for Grand Slams [Top 1000]," baseball-almanac.com, http://www.baseball-almanac.com/hitting/higs1.shtml [25 June 2018].
7. Scott Ostler, "Canseco Really Appreciates a Good Bash, Even One by Gibson," latimes.com, http://articles.latimes.com/1988-10-16/sports/sp-6722_1_jose-canseco [27 June 2018].
8. "Tim Belcher talks about his Kansas City days, the 1988 World Series with the Dodgers and Zack Greinke," royals.mlbblogs.com, https://royals.mlblogs.com/tim-belcher-talks-about-his-kansas-city-days-the-1988-world-series-with-the-dodgers-and-zack-greinke-945aff7135a2 [9 June 2018].

CHAPTER 6: THE PRELUDE

1. Lyle Spencer, "Oral History of Epic Mets-Dodgers 1988 NLCS," mlb.com, https://www.mlb.com/news/oral-history-of-epic-mets-dodgers-1988-nlcs/c-152995440 [18 July 018].

2. Ibid.
3. Bill Plaschke, "It's No Act," *Los Angeles Times*, 14 October 1988, 60.
4. Ibid.
5. Shirley Povich, "An Old Ghost Might've Headed Cone Off," Washingtonpost.com, https://www.washingtonpost.com/archive/sports/1988/10/09/an-old-ghost-mightve-headed-cone-off/9f65432e-a127-499f-a39e-c3ea04bb554a/?noredirect=on&utm_term=.b7f6024c29e6, [9 October 1988].
6. Dave Carpenter, "Oakland's Baylor Unloads a Blast Toward Dodger Pitcher Howell," deseretnews.com [Associated Press], https://www.deseretnews.com/article/20603/Oaklands-Baylor-Unloads-A-Blast-Toward-Dodger-Pitcher-Howell----Oaklands-Baylor-Unloads-A-Blast.html [15 October 1988].
7. Ibid.
8. Ibid.

CHAPTER 8: BEFORE THE STORM

1. Sam McManis, "Dodgers Selling Chances Short; A's Don't Buy It," *Los Angeles Times*, 15 October 2018, 20.
2. Ibid., 59.
3. Ibid.

CHAPTER 10: THE BATBOY

1. "Tommy Lasorda," baseballhall.org, https://baseballhall.org/hall-of-famers/lasorda-tommy [16 July 2018].
2. "Tommy Lasorda's Hall of Fame Induction Speech," archivedinnings.com, https://archivedinnings.com/2016/09/11/tommy-lasordas-hall-of-fame-induction-speech/ [17 July 2018].
3. "Managers With the Most World Series Championships," foxsports.com, https://www.foxsports.com/mlb/gallery/managers-most-world-series-titles-mccarthy-stengel-mack-bochy-la-russa-sparky-alston-torre-110114 [17 July 2019].
4. "That was a cool feeling': An oral history of Kirk Gibson's iconic 1988 home run," si.com, https://www.si.com/mlb/strike-zone/2013/10/15/kirk-gibson-dennis-eckersley-dodgers-athletics-1988-world-series-home-run-oral-history [18 July 2018].
5. Ibid.
6. Arash Markazi, "'It's a Good Story': Inside Kirk Gibson's epic 1988 World Series HR," espn.com, http://www.espn.com/mlb/story/_/id/24974235/mlb-kirk-gibson-world-series-home-run-30-years-later [17 December 2018].

INDEX

Aaron, Hank, xviii, xxi
Albany-Colonie A's, 21
Albuquerque Dodgers, 38
American League, xiv–xvi, xxiii, 14–15, 32, 43, 47–48, 50, 54, 56–57, 60, 73, 97, 109, 119–20, 127, 130, 132
American League Championship Series, 48, 50, 54, 73, 79, 83, 97, 120
Amoros, Sandy, xviii
Alston, Walt, 90
Amalfitano, Joe, xv, 32, 39, 109–10, 113, 116, 118
American Legion, 106, 121
Anaheim Angels, 13, 22
Anderson, Dave, 103–104
Anderson, Sparky, 90
Arellano, Jason, 35
Arizona Diamondbacks, 126, 130
Arizona State University, vii
Atlanta Braves, 48

Baltimore Orioles, 47, 81, 132
Barber, Red, xxi
Baylor, Don, 37, 67–68
Beckett, Josh, 9
Belcher, Tim, xiv, 13, 18–28, 35–36, 46–52, 54–55, 57–61, 64–66, 68, 72, 74, 79–80, 86, 92, 122
Bellingham Dodgers, 31
Berra, Yogi, xx, 54
Berry, Ken, 87
Big 10 Conference, 106
Boston Braves, xxi
Boston Red Sox, x, xxiii, 33, 48, 54, 57, 75, 83, 87, 96, 127
Branca, Ralph, xxii, xxiv, 59
Brooklyn Dodgers, xviii–xix, xxi, xxvi, 7, 16, 89, 113, 130

Brooklyn Robins, 54
Bush, Vice-president George H.W., 65

Cadaret, Greg, 35, 85–86, 117, 119
California Angels, 54, 97
Cameron, Mike, 122
Campanella, Roy, xviii
Canseco Jr., Jose, xi, xxi, xxiv, 1, 14, 24–27, 32, 34, 36, 43, 45–47, 50–51, 53, 55–60, 62, 64, 68–69, 74–76, 81, 83–84, 97–98, 111, 113, 120, 132
Canseco Sr., Jose, 56
Canseco, Ozzie, 56
[Capas] Canseco, Barbara, 56
Castro, Fidel, 56
CBS Radio, xix, 2
Chavez Ravine, xvii, xxi, xxvi, 7
Chicago Cubs, 7, 9, 18, 96, 124
Chicago Tribune, 121
Chicago White Sox, 22, 56, 129, 130, 148
Cincinnati Reds, xix, xxiii, 18, 22, 32
Claire, Fred, 10, 21, 31, 36, 39, 64, 68, 91, 97, 102, 114, 118, 127
Cleveland Indians, 53, 95–97
Clinton Dodgers, 31, 38
Colias, Susan, 77
College World Series, vii, ix, 120
Concord Weavers, 89
Cone, David, 4, 67
Coral Park High School, 56
Costas, Bob, 11, 117
Cousins, Derryl, 40
Cy Young Award, xx, xxiv, 9, 15, 23, 90, 95–96

Danville Dodgers, 31
Darling, Ron, 4, 97
Davis, Mark, 23
Davis, Mike, xxvii, 1, 10, 68, 94, 101–103, 107–11, 115, 117–19, 122
Davis, Tommy, xx
Dedeaux, Rod, viii–x, 15
Dempsey, Rick, 10, 47, 61, 85, 109, 119, 134
Dennis Eckersley Field, 127
Desmond, Connie, xxi
Detroit Tigers, xxv, 14, 22, 106, 120, 126
Didier, Mel, 110–11, 116
Dodger Stadium, vii, ix, xi, xiii, xvii–xxi, xxv–xxvi, 1–2, 7, 9–10, 18–20, 24, 32, 34–35, 40, 54–55, 59, 69, 71, 74, 84, 88–89, 91–92, 104, 115–16, 118, 129
Doggett, Jerry, xviii, 9
Dondanville, Craig, 2
Dondanville, Scott, 87
Duncan, Dave, 85
Durocher, Leo, 91
Drysdale, Don, xx, 22, 123

Ebbets Field, ix, 8
Eckersley, Dennis, ix, xxi, xxiii–xxiv, 1, 23, 29, 45, 70, 87, 95–93, 99, 100–103, 105, 107–11, 115–19, 121, 123, 125–28
Erskine, Carl, xviii, xxvi, 59, 105
Evansville Triplets, 106

Fairly, Ron, xviii
Fenway Park, 7
Fernandez, Sid, 4
Fisk, Carlton, x, xxiii, xxv, 91
Forbes Field, xxiii

INDEX

Ford C. Frick Award, xxvi, 130
Ford, Whitey, xx
Fordham University, 8
Fox Sports Net Detroit, 126
Frick, Ford, xxvi, 130
Furillo, Carl, xviii

Gallego, Mike, 48–49
Garagiola, Joe, 2, 67
Garvey, Steve, 8
Giamatti, Bart, 66
Gibson, Barbara, 105
Gibson, Bob, 105
Gibson, Debbie, 2
Gibson, Kirk, ix–xvii,
  xx–xxiv, xxvi–xxvii, 1,
  4–7, 10–11, 13–14, 17,
  19, 23, 29–30, 33–35,
  45–46, 62, 64, 70–71,
  74–78, 80, 82, 85,
  87–88, 92–95, 98–99,
  101–127, 130–34
Gilliam, Jim, xviii
Gooden, Dwight, 4–5, 27,
  63, 99
Grace, Mark, 18
Green, Shawn, xvi
Greenville Spinners, 89
Griffin, Alfredo, 10, 13, 48,
  61, 68, 72, 74–75, 83,
  101, 118
Grimes, Burleigh, 53
Gross, Kevin, 9
Gwynn, Tony, 13

Hamilton, Jeff, 13, 72, 85,
  100–101
Hassey, Ron, 107–10
Hatcher, Mickey, xi, xiv, 1,
  6, 12, 35, 37–45, 48–49,
  52, 68, 72–75, 79, 81,
  83–84, 122
Harvey, Doug, 20, 23, 25,
  27, 36, 43, 50, 52
Heep, Danny, 68
Henderson, Dave, 14,
  23–24, 26, 37, 46, 51,
  54, 75–76, 81, 84
Herbert Hoover High
  School, 102

Hershiser, Orel, 4–6, 10, 18,
  32–33, 64, 70, 73, 83, 95,
  103, 107, 116, 122, 125
Highland High School, 21
Hines, Ben, 10, 26, 41, 59,
  94, 104, 113, 117
Hodges, Gil, xviii, xxi
Hodges, Russ, xxii
Holman Stadium, xvii
Honeycutt, Rick, 21, 32, 64,
  92, 119–21
Horton, Ricky, 19, 60, 85,
  104, 125
Houston Astros, 37, 54, 148
Howard, Elston, xx
Howard, Frank, xviii
Howe, Steve, 8
Howell, Jay, 5, 10, 37,
  66–68, 104, 124
Hubbard, Glenn, 15, 47–51,
  59–60, 72
Huntsville Stars, 21, 57

Idaho Falls A's, 56

Javier, Stan, 24, 86
Johnson, Darrell, 91
Jones, Careen, 18

Kansas City Athletics, 16,
  89, 125–26
Kansas City Royals, 22, 126
Kennedy, President John F.,
  viii, 7
Kennedy, Robert F., viii
Kershaw, Clayton, 9, 71
Kettering High School, 105
KFI Radio, xviii
Kirk Gibson Foundation,
  125–26
Koufax, Sandy, xix–xx, 9,
  29, 90
Kuehfuss, Brad, 5, 46
Kuehn, Harvey, xix
Kuehner, Pat, vii–viii, xi,
  120–21

Labine, Clem, xviii
Lachemann, Rene, 19–20,
  103, 111, 113

Lachemann, Laurie, 113
Lakeland Flying Tigers, 106
Lansford, Carney, 14, 19–20,
  23, 26–27, 51–52,
  59–60, 74, 81, 85, 122,
  129
LaRussa, Tony, 15–16, 19,
  33, 51, 72, 74, 79, 85,
  91, 95, 105, 110, 113,
  123, 129–30
Lasorda, Carmella, 88
Lasorda, Jo, 91
Lasorda, Sabatino, 88
Lasorda, Tommy, x, 1,
  6–7, 11, 13–16, 25,
  32, 39, 41, 46, 51–52,
  54–55, 60, 64, 67–68,
  74–76, 89–94, 100–105,
  108–109, 113, 115, 118,
  124–25, 129–31
Lasorda, Tom Jr., 129
Lazzeri, Tony, 54
Leary, Tim, 18, 52, 54,
  60, 66, 71–72, 74–76,
  80–81, 83, 92
Lefebvre, Jim, 19–20
Life and News, 120
Lifetime Achievement Emmy
  Award, 130
Los Angeles Angels, 8
Los Angeles Dodgers, ix–xi,
  xvii, xix–xxi, xxiv–xxv,
  xxvii, 2–10, 12–22,
  24–25, 28–45, 47–50,
  54–55, 59, 61–72,
  74–95, 97, 99, 101–103,
  105–107, 109–10, 113,
  115, 120–23, 125–26,
  129–30, 132–33
Los Angeles Memorial
  Coliseum, xix, 7
Los Angeles Times, 6, 41, 121

Mack, Connie, 130
Madison Muskies, 21
Mantle, Mickey, xx, 154
Maris, Roger, xx
Marshall, Mike, xxiv, 4,
  12–13, 43, 75, 84–85,
  122

Martinez, Ramon, 9
Matthews, Eddie, xviii
Mazeroski, Bill, x–xi, xxiii–xxv, xxvii, 91, 116–17
McCarthy, Joe, 91
McDougald, Gil, 54
McGraw, John, 130
McGwire, Mark, xxiv–xxv, 15, 24, 26–27, 32, 34, 44–47, 49–51, 60, 68, 76, 78, 85, 97, 107, 122, 132–33
Merkley, Glade, 30
Merkley, Keith, 71
Merrill, Durwood, 37
Mesa Community College, 37
Mesa High School, 37
Miami Marlins [Class A], 56
Michigan State University, 11, 106, 114, 119
Milwaukee Braves, xviii
Milwaukee Brewers, xxi, 19
Minnesota Twins, xxvii, 21, 38
Modesto A's, 102
Moore, Donnie, 54
Mota, Manny, 107
Mount Vernon Nazarene University, 21–22, 25
Murtaugh, Danny, 91

National Baseball Hall of Fame, x, xxi, 16, 24, 26, 32–33, 36, 40, 53–54, 56, 90, 96–97, 114, 128, 130
National Collegiate Athletic Association, vii
National League, xviii, xxiv–xxvi, 6–7, 10, 13–15, 23, 26, 32, 90, 102, 109, 116
National League Championship Series, xxiv, 4, 13, 18, 21, 23, 33, 48, 62–64, 71, 74, 77, 99, 101, 103, 120
National League Division Series, 50

National League West Division, 10, 18, 126
Nelson, Gene, 85
Newcombe, Don, 59
New York Giants, xxi, xxii, 42
New York Mets, 3–6, 18, 27, 33–34, 37, 41, 43–44, 48, 54, 62–64, 66, 71, 73, 77–79, 83, 99, 120–21
New York Times, 121
New York Yankees, x, xxvii, 21, 54, 57, 90–91
Nomo, Hideo, 9
Noren, Irv, xviii, xxv–xxvi

Oakland A's, ix, xi, xx–xxi, xxiii–xxv, xxvii, 2, 10, 15–16, 18–19, 21, 23–24, 27–32, 35, 42, 44, 47–51, 53, 55–56, 58–64, 66–68, 71–72, 75, 78–81, 83–87, 95–97, 102, 107, 109–10, 115, 117–19, 121–22, 125, 127, 129–30
Oates, Johnny, 96
Ojeda, Bob, 4
O'Malley, Peter, 91
O'Malley, Walter, xxvi, 8
Orbison, Roy, 66
Orosco, Jesse, 10, 104, 124
Ostler, Scott, 6, 41

Pafko, Andy, 32, 113
Park, Chan Ho, 23
Parker, Dave, 14, 24, 26–27, 40, 51, 60, 75, 86
Pasadena City College, 93
Peabody, Ross, 63
Pena, Alejandro, 86, 92, 97, 104, 132
Perranoski, Ron, 46, 50, 52, 55, 75
Philadelphia Phillies, 30, 32, 89, 147
Phillips, Tony, 48, 125

Piazza, Mike, 24
Pitlock, Skip, ix
Pittsburgh Pirates, x, xxiii–xxiv, 26
Podres, Johnny, xix, 8
Polo Grounds, xxi, 113
Poole, Mitch, 19, 88, 93–98, 132–33

Quinn, Bob, 96

Reagan, Nancy, 4
Reagan, President Ronald, 65
Reese, Pee Wee, 90
Reuss, Jerry, 9, 39
Richardson, Bobby, 54
Rogers, Darryl, 106
Roseboro, John, xviii
Ruth, Babe, xxi

Sabo, Chris, 18
St. Elizabeth's High School, 31
St. Louis Cardinals, 16, 48, 96, 125, 139
San Antonio Dodgers, 31, 38
San Diego Padres, 23
San Diego State University, 48
San Francisco Giants, xix
Sax, Steve, 5, 12, 35–36, 40–41, 43, 48, 61, 75, 86, 109, 116
Schenectady Blue Jays, 89
Schmidt, Mike, 40
Scioscia, Mike, 5, 12, 19, 47, 50, 52, 54, 58, 61, 63–65, 84–85, 99–101
Scully, Joan, 130
Scully, Michael, 130
Scully, Vin, xvii, xix–xxii, xxvi, 1–2, 4, 6–9, 33, 58–59, 93–93, 97, 104, 112–13, 117, 122–23, 130–31
Seattle Mariners, 22, 65
Shea Stadium, 5, 64
Shelby, John, 12, 27, 43–44, 46, 58–59, 63, 73, 84–85

INDEX 155

Singer, Bill, 9
Smith, Elmer, 53
Snider, Duke, xviii
Southern Illinois University, ix
Sparta High School, 18
Sporting News, 21
Stanton, Giancarlo, 24
Stargell, Willie, 24
Stengel, Casey, 91
Steinbach, Terry, 15, 24, 27, 40, 46, 72, 76
Steinbeck, John, 7, 69
Stewart, Dave, xxiv, 15–16, 30–32, 35–37, 40, 43–44, 47–48, 50–52, 59–60, 68, 74, 76, 80–81, 83–86, 92, 95, 99
Strawberry, Darryl, 4, 13, 63
Stubbs, Franklin, 12, 37, 73–76
Suchon, Josh, 120
Switzer, Barry, 37

Tacoma Tigers, 21, 57
Terry, Ralph, xxiv
Texas League, 96
Texas Rangers, 30, 57
The Natural, 116
Thomson, Bobby, x–xiii, xxiv–xxvi, 59, 91, 105, 113, 117, 123
Toronto Blue Jays, 32

University of North Carolina, 50
University of Oklahoma, 37
University of Southern California, vii–viii, 78, 131, 133

Valenzuela, Fernando, 9
Virdon, Bill, xxvii, 116

Wagner, Evan, 3, 83
Wagner, Rob, 2, 3
Washington Union High School, 95

Weiss, Walt, 15, 47, 49–50, 68, 72–73, 99
Waterbury A's, 102
White, Bill, 2
Willett, Kathy, 99
Williams, Dick, 65
Wills, Maury, xviii, xx
Woodson, Tracy, 72, 80
World Series, vii, ix–xi, xix, xx–xxi, xxiii, xxv, xxvii, 1–4, 6, 8, 10–11, 13–14, 17, 18–23, 26, 30–33, 35–36, 39, 41–43, 45, 47–55, 61–68, 70–72, 74–75, 77, 79–81, 84, 87–88, 90–91, 93–94, 98, 101–102, 104–105, 115–16, 120–22, 125–27, 129–34
Wrigley Field [Chicago], 7
Wrigley Field [Los Angeles], 8

Yeager, Steve, 8, 65

ABOUT THE AUTHOR

Steven K. Wagner rose from car wash attendant to write for the legendary wire service United Press International (UPI) and eventually become a baseball historian. The author of four books, Mr. Wagner is among the most prolific baseball authors over the past decade. He began his career as a staff writer and assistant bureau chief with UPI. He then joined *The Oregonian* as the Portland newspaper's Vancouver, Washington, bureau chief—working as a lead writer covering the eruption of Mount St. Helens—and later as the paper's night crime reporter. Over the past 30 years the author, a former editor of the Los Angeles Rams' team magazine, has freelanced extensively for the *Los Angeles Times*. His work also has appeared in the *New York Times, Washington Post, Seattle Times, Oklahoma City Oklahoman, Portland Tribune, Baseball America,* and many other newspapers and magazines. Mr. Wagner has been married for 31 years, has two grown children, and resides in Southeast Pennsylvania.

Steven Wagner (© Hannah E. Larkin)

Made in the USA
Las Vegas, NV
20 April 2022